THE FLOW
of
FIVE TIERS

A Framework for Structuring High-Functioning Organizations

by

KENNETH PEARSON

SCARMORA
PRESS

*Dedicated to those who believe work
can be a place of purpose, growth, and dignity -
and who show up every day to make that belief a reality.*

THE FLOW OF FIVE TIERS

Send all inquiries to the following address:

Scarmora Press
17630 South Bronze Mountain Pass
Vail, AZ 85641
www.scarmorapress.com
www.pearsonpearson.llc

*Scarmora Press is a subsidiary of Pearson & Pearson LLC.

First Edition
Printed in the United States of America
ISBN: 978-0-9768543-4-0

TABLE OF CONTENTS

INTRODUCTION

BUILDING THE STRUCTURE THAT HOLDS US TOGETHER

There comes a moment in every organization's life when the scaffolding that once held everything together begins to strain, when momentum feels like motion without meaning, and even the most well-intentioned leaders begin to sense a quiet drift. Not a collapse, not a crisis, but a subtle unraveling. Decisions lose cohesion. Values become ornamental. Feedback echoes without response. The work continues, but the why begins to blur.

If you've ever felt that drift, if you've ever stood in a meeting wondering how your team became so misaligned, reviewed a strategic plan that no one references anymore, or felt the growing fatigue of employees who care deeply but no longer know what direction to face, then this book is for you.

The Flow of Five Tiers is not a one-size-fits-all solution. It is a framework. A foundation. A map that doesn't prescribe your path, but helps you draw it with intention. At its core, this is a book about structure – not the rigid, bureaucratic kind that stifles creativity, but the living kind that gives shape to purpose, direction to leadership, and rhythm to change. It's about how organizations can be built to move, to learn, to grow, without losing their soul along the way.

Across these pages, you'll explore five interdependent tiers that together create the architecture of a resilient, values-driven organization.

Tier 1: Foundational Core is where it all begins. This is your purpose, your vision, your values, and your governance. This isn't about branding statements or laminated slogans; it's about anchoring every decision, every policy, and every behavior to a shared reason for being. A strong foundation ensures that people know not just what they're doing, but why it matters, and how it connects to the bigger picture.

Tier 2: Leadership & Strategy brings that foundation to life through aligned leadership. It examines what happens when leaders operate in isolation versus when they function as a system. This tier helps organizations build leadership clarity, define decision-making pathways, and align departmental goals with enterprise-wide purpose. Because without structural cohesion at the top, even the most inspiring missions fragment under pressure.

Tier 3: Culture & People turns values into lived experience. It looks at how behavior is modeled, how culture is reinforced (or neglected), and how organizations can create environments where people feel safe, respected, and empowered to contribute. This tier holds the pulse of the organization and challenges us to design for productivity, belonging, development, and trust.

Tier 4: Processes & Systems is where operational integrity is built. It's the structure that either enables flow or obstructs it. This tier helps identify when bureaucracy overwhelms purpose and when systems have become barriers rather than bridges, and offers tools to streamline, clarify, and realign workflows with values and mission. Because even the best talent cannot succeed in a broken system.

Tier 5: Impact & Outcomes is the culmination, the mirror that reflects whether your organization is merely performing or truly evolving. This tier explores how feedback becomes action, how improvement becomes embedded, and how curiosity becomes a competency. It's about learning in real time, responding with agility, and designing systems that never stop improving because they never stop listening.

Each tier in this framework stands on its own, yet none exist in isolation. They are part of a living ecosystem. A weakness in one creates pressure in the others. A strength in one can cascade into new possibilities across the whole. This book doesn't ask you to fix everything at once. Instead, it invites you to begin, wherever you are, with the tier that calls you most.

What you'll find in the chapters ahead are not abstract theories, but lived realities, stories of organizations that faltered, systems that calcified, cultures that fractured, and the people who worked to restore alignment, clarity, and care. You'll also find the tools to help you do the same. Each chapter moves through a structure: a story to ground the concept, a breakdown of what's really happening beneath the surface, integration guidance to show how it fits into the broader system, implementation strategies to bring it to life, and practical tools and questions to take with you.

This is the work of building what lasts.

And make no mistake, structure matters. Not because it restricts, but because it holds. It is what allows people to do their best work without having to fight the system to do it. It's what makes values real, not rhetorical. It's what transforms organizations from good intentions into sustained impact.

In a world that is moving faster than ever, the temptation is to chase tactics. But before you redesign your brand, overhaul your hiring strategy, or launch a new initiative, pause. Ask the deeper question: What structure are we building on? Because even the most visionary ideas will collapse if they rest on sand.

So let this be your foundation. Your framework.

Not a prescription, but a practice. Not the answer, but a path toward better questions.

Let this be where your flow begins.

11

TIER 1: FOUNDATIONAL CORE

Establishing Purpose, Vision, Policies, & Governance

CHAPTER 1

THE MISSING BLUEPRINT

Why Organizations Struggle without a Clear Foundation

THE STORY OF ELENA

Before the collapse, everything appeared ... fine. On the surface, Northbend Community Alliance presented itself as a stable, productive nonprofit. Quarterly performance metrics met expectations. Staff arrived on time, responded to emails, attended meetings, and completed tasks. There were no glaring red flags, no lawsuits, public scandals, or financial disasters. Yet something elusive, something essential, was unraveling beneath the surface. The collapse, when it came, wasn't explosive. It was quiet, cumulative, and suffocating.

Elena Alvarez, freshly appointed as Director of Operations, was only a few weeks into her tenure when she began to sense it. It wasn't a single moment, but a lingering discomfort, an organizational inertia masked as productivity. She couldn't quite put her finger on it until the first leadership team meeting. There, five department heads gathered around a glossy table and debated the organization's top priorities. One lobbied for a robust national expansion strategy. Another emphasized deepening local community partnerships. A third focused on enhancing internal systems. Each spoke eloquently, confidently, passionately even. Their visions were compelling, but none of them aligned. The meeting ended with courteous nods and an unspoken unease. Elena paused before closing her notebook and asked what she thought was a basic question: "What exactly are we trying to achieve over the next two years?"

Silence. Not the reflective kind. This was the stunned kind, heavy and loud. Finally, someone offered a tentative goal. Then another chimed in with something completely different. A third diverged even further. There were no lies or fabrications, just fractured truths. Each answer was rooted in personal interpretation, not in any shared understanding.

Seeking clarity, Elena asked to review the strategic plan. What she received was a five-year-old PowerPoint file littered with vague catchphrases like *Move the Needle* and *Ignite Community Impact*. It was filled with jargon, but devoid of direction. She pressed further, requesting the organization's mission. She received three versions: one was etched into a wooden plaque at the building's entrance, another printed in the employee handbook, and a third prominently displayed on the website. They shared a general spirit, but each told a slightly different story. Which one was true?

The deeper she went, the more unsettling the patterns became. Departments were making decisions in isolation. Priorities clashed. Policies were enforced inconsistently, sometimes contradicting one another. Employees who were bright, passionate, and capable, appeared increasingly weary. Not apathetic, but confused. Their disengagement wasn't the result of disinterest. It came from uncertainty. No one could say for sure what mattered most. Everyone was rowing, but in different directions. It wasn't a lack of leadership. It was the absence of something more elemental. It was the absence of a blueprint.

After one particularly chaotic planning session, Elena lingered in the conference room, staring at a whiteboard covered in a tangle of ideas, half-erased initiatives, and arrows that led nowhere. It looked like a map drawn by multiple cartographers, each with a different destination in mind. That was the moment of realization: without a common language of purpose, without a blueprint that anchored identity and intention, even the most committed teams would drift. Leadership was not enough. Passion was not enough. In the absence of clarity, chaos had taken root.

The Strategic Lens

Elena's experience is not unique. It echoes a broader reality for many organizations: the erosion of clarity often masquerades as stability. The first step in resolving this is not to leap into rewriting a mission statement or restructuring departments. Instead, it's about elevating our vantage point – stepping back to examine how foundational elements are functioning, or failing to function, across the organization.

Ask yourself: Does everyone in the organization understand and agree upon its purpose? Not in the form of memorized taglines, but through a shared ability to explain why the organization exists, who it serves, and what it aims to accomplish. If answers vary wildly, it's a sign that purpose has become interpretive rather than unified.

Consider whether your vision is an active compass or a forgotten phrase. If strategic efforts feel disjointed or reactive, chances are your vision isn't doing the work it's meant to do. It should be the framework that connects initiatives across the organization and offers continuity during change.

Look at your stated values and ask: Where are they visible in our everyday behavior? Are they upheld in performance evaluations, conflict resolution, and team collaboration? Or do they live only on posters and introductory slides?

When values aren't integrated into how people actually work together, the gap between who we say we are and who we show up as begins to widen.

Then, examine governance. How are decisions made, and by whom? If policies are inconsistently enforced or decision-making feels arbitrary, the problem may not be the people. The problem may be the structure. Governance should be clear, fair, and aligned with both mission and values. If employees can't trace decisions back to transparent processes or accountable leaders, trust falters.

These questions aren't academic, they're diagnostic. They help expose the quiet fractures that, over time, can compromise even the most promising organizations. But they also create space to reconnect. To pause the rush and return to what holds an organization together – shared identity, directional clarity, and principled action. The blueprint isn't a document. It's a collective way of knowing and doing. When that knowing is clear, organizations move with purpose. When it's missing, even the most well-intentioned efforts will lead nowhere.

Structural Insights

What Elena discovered at Northbend is a common but often unspoken truth. Many organizations operate without a coherent foundation. They rely on momentum, habit, and charisma – on legacy programs or the distinctive styles of individual leaders – to keep things moving. But when that foundation is fragmented, or worse, nonexistent, the cracks do not appear all at once. They emerge quietly: misaligned goals, competing priorities, disengaged staff, and a creeping sense of disconnection. Over time, these fractures deepen, weakening the organization's resilience and unity.

Tier 1: Foundational Core of the *Five Tiers Framework* is where the organization's identity, direction, and commitments reside. It includes three essential elements: mission, vision, and values. These are not abstract ideals or branding slogans; they are the organization's structural DNA. The mission answers the foundational question: Why do we exist? It articulates the promise the organization makes to its stakeholders and communities. The vision projects where the organization aspires to go, a vivid image of the future it seeks to co-create. Values serve as the compass, guiding how the organization will behave, make decisions, and build relationships on that journey.

When clearly defined and genuinely integrated, these components do more than decorate a lobby wall. They become active forces, anchoring decision-making, unifying teams, and orienting the organization during times of change. They are the lenses through which every policy is evaluated, every program is designed, and every conversation about culture is held. But when these components are neglected – left vague, contradictory, or stale – they become liabilities. They confuse more than clarify. They erode trust. They sabotage alignment. And most dangerously, they create the illusion of cohesion where none exists.

Equally important are the foundational structures of governance and policy. If the mission and values are the "why" and "what," governance represents the "who decides" and "how." Effective governance clarifies authority, decision rights, and accountability across the organization. It ensures that power is distributed with intention and that leadership responsibilities are transparent and just. Policies, in turn, operationalize values. A stated commitment to equity must be visible in hiring processes, compensation systems, disciplinary protocols, and advancement pathways. Otherwise, values remain performative rather than transformative.

To be foundational, then, is not simply to exist at the beginning, but to support everything else that follows. It is about creating a deep, consistent identity that can be trusted, referenced, and built upon.

Cross-Tier Impact

The **Foundational Core** is not an isolated tier. It is the bloodstream of the entire *Five Tiers Framework*. When mission, vision, and values are clear, alive, and aligned, each subsequent tier of the organization becomes easier to shape with purpose. In **Tier 2**, strategy becomes cohesive rather than fragmented. Leaders aren't just chasing growth or innovation, they're doing so in a way that reflects who they are and what they stand for. Strategic initiatives are filtered through core values, which act as ethical guardrails and directional compasses.

Leadership development in **Tier 3** is no longer generic. It becomes mission-driven. Leaders are not simply trained in competencies, they are cultivated to embody and model the values of the organization. Talent development isn't just about filling roles; it's about building continuity of purpose. Onboarding becomes storytelling. Succession planning becomes philosophical alignment. The transfer of knowledge becomes the transfer of culture.

By **Tier 4**, the foundational tier becomes embedded in operations. Policies, workflows, systems of accountability, and even the customer or client experience begin to reflect the organization's identity. Performance indicators are shaped by purpose, not just output. Service standards are infused with values. Internal systems are designed to affirm the organization's deepest commitments.

And in **Tier 5**, the foundation becomes a reference point for all adaptation and growth. Feedback loops don't just measure productivity; they evaluate integrity. Continuous improvement isn't adrift. It's tethered. Innovation doesn't chase novelty, it evolves with intention. The organization remains agile, but not aimless.

Without this core, the entire system falters. Strategy becomes reactive. Culture becomes confused. Leadership becomes inconsistent. And improvement becomes disjointed. But with a well-formed, living foundation, the organization becomes centered, adaptable, and unmistakably whole.

Designing the Shift

Establishing **Tier 1** begins with clarity, but its durability comes from design. It's not enough to revise a mission statement or reprint a values poster. Real transformation begins by asking courageous questions: Who are we? Why do we exist? What do we believe in, especially when tested? What future are we committed to building?

These are not questions that can be answered in a single leadership retreat. They require inclusive dialogue, active listening, and honest reflection. Organizational Development professionals play a critical role here, guiding leaders through interviews, focus groups, and workshops designed to uncover the organization's core truths. This is not a branding exercise. It is a discovery process of identity, purpose, and responsibility.

Once refined, the mission, vision, and values must be embedded, not shelved. They must show up in recruitment materials, job descriptions, onboarding programs, and team charters. They must shape how leaders are evaluated and how difficult decisions are made. Governance models should reflect them. Policies should be tested against them. They must be both visible and felt.

This is an ongoing practice. Implementation is not a launch. Implementation is a rhythm. It requires auditing existing systems for contradictions, holding leaders accountable to the values they espouse, and creating rituals that keep the foundation alive. Whether it's monthly reflections, annual planning reviews, or leadership check-ins, the foundation must be kept visible, useful, and honored.

Operationalizing Change

Begin with awareness, not answers. Ask yourself and your team: Can most employees name the mission? Can they explain how values show up in daily decisions? Is the vision reflected in where the organization invests time and energy? If not, begin the work, not with a rewrite, but with a conversation.

Host a leadership alignment session. Explore discrepancies. Identify themes. Facilitate employee focus groups. Share initial findings. Make revisions transparent. Invite feedback not just as a formality, but as a value in action.

Then, bring it to life. Turn values into competencies. Integrate mission into your performance management system. Shape strategic planning with the vision as your north star. Review governance structures for clarity and consistency. Align compensation, hiring, and promotion practices with what the organization says it values and represents.

And finally, establish rhythm. Make the **Foundational Core** part of the organizational heartbeat. Incorporate it into team meetings. Use it to frame leadership development. Revisit it annually and during moments of change. Introduce it to every new employee as information, and as an invitation to belong, to contribute, and to believe.

Executive Takeawyas
Tier 1: Foundational Core is not an abstract concept. It is the unseen architecture that determines whether an organization flourishes or falters. Without it, even the most skilled teams lose direction, even the most inspiring visions fail to take root. But with it, the organization gains coherence, integrity, and the power to grow with intention.

This tier is not simply something to define. This tier is something to live. It is found in how decisions are made, how policies are written, how conflicts are resolved, and how people are treated. It is the space where meaning and method intertwine. It is the beginning, but also the throughline, of everything that follows.

Chapter 1: Leadership Checkpoints

- What is our organization's true purpose, and is it clearly articulated across all levels?
- Can we name our core values, and more importantly, can we describe how we live them out in practice?
- When was the last time we evaluated whether our mission, vision, and values still reflect who we are today?
- Do our governance and policy structures reflect our values, or contradict them?
- How do we ensure that new employees are introduced to our foundational elements in a meaningful, lasting way?
- Are our leaders aligned in their understanding of our direction, or are they pulling in different directions?
- What would it take to bring our foundational tier out of the background and into daily operation?

CHAPTER 2

THE HOUSE BUILT ON SAND

The Danger of Misaligned Values

THE STORY OF OLIVIA

At first, it was easy to dismiss. The slight eye rolls in meetings, the side glances after decisions, the polite but pointed silence when leadership asked for input. Olivia Morris, Chief People Officer at BrightForm Tech, knew how to spot cultural signals. She had spent two decades studying the subtle alchemy of organizational behavior. And still, she wasn't prepared for how deeply the foundation had cracked.

When Olivia joined BrightForm, the company was rising fast, admired for both its innovation and its humanity. Values like *People First* and *Integrity Always* were more than statements. They were a presence. They greeted employees on "Day One" through orientation, echoed in town hall meetings, and were printed on t-shirts proudly worn by new hires and executives alike. Olivia believed in the mission and admired the leadership's vision. But as the company scaled, something started to shift. It wasn't immediate. The shift was insidious.

After a particularly demanding product cycle, she noticed corners being cut. Not maliciously, but methodically. A senior engineer known for his collaborative spirit was suddenly passed over for promotion in favor of a high-performer with sharp metrics and a sharp tongue. "We need people who drive numbers," someone had said. Then came the dismissal of a beloved manager with no communication or transparency. In his place came someone who had experience leading profitable teams, but whose interpersonal style left many team members wary. The company line was, "It's a necessary move to support growth." But to those watching, it felt like a betrayal of everything they'd been told to believe in.

The final rupture came with a new attendance policy. It landed with no warning, no consultation. Gone were the flexible arrangements that had helped build trust. In their place was a rigid, impersonal policy emphasizing compliance over care. The reasoning was vague – "business needs" – but the message was clear. Trust was no longer assumed. Autonomy was no longer honored. Within hours, employee Slack channels were buzzing. Not with outrage, but with disappointment. Olivia watched in real-time as morale eroded. It wasn't the policy itself that broke people's hearts. It was the clarity of the contradiction. The story they had believed in, the one printed on mugs and walls, was no longer true.

Olivia brought her concerns to the executive team. They nodded sympathetically, offered reassurances, and moved on to the next agenda item. And that was the moment she knew. The values had become a costume – a carefully curated image worn for external perception. But beneath the surface, the soul of the organization was fading. And the people felt it.

The Strategic Lens

Olivia's story doesn't begin with a crisis. Her story begins with dissonance. Not loud enough to set off alarms, but present enough to shift the emotional climate. A promotion that contradicts stated values. A policy rolled out with no dialogue. A slow drift from "people first" to "performance at any cost." These are the signs of a foundation starting to crack. A foundation cracking because values were no longer protected.

To understand whether your organization is facing a similar erosion, step back and examine how values are functioning not just as ideals, but as operating principles.

Start by asking: Are your organizational values still trusted?

Not just repeated, but believed. Do employees experience them as real, or do they view them as marketing language disconnected from daily decisions? Olivia noticed the shift not through a formal announcement, but through changed behaviors – people hesitating to speak up, managers emphasizing compliance over care. These aren't surface-level changes. They're symptoms of a deeper misalignment.

Next, consider how leadership handles contradiction. When policies or promotions seem at odds with stated values, is there space for dialogue? Or is discomfort quietly redirected or ignored? Olivia's executive team didn't deny the values. They simply didn't defend them. In that silence, the message was clear: values were negotiable.

Think about how power is exercised in your organization. Do leaders model the values under pressure, or only when convenient? A flexible attendance policy, once celebrated as a trust-building tool, was replaced with rigid compliance. It wasn't the change that broke trust. It was the way the change was introduced. When values are left out of the decision-making process, employees begin to question whether they were ever real to begin with.

Finally, assess where your values live. Are they part of your hiring rubric? Do they appear in how performance is evaluated, or in how conflict is resolved? Or do they live primarily in aspirational slide decks and printed merchandise? In Olivia's case, the values hadn't disappeared. They had just stopped showing up where they mattered.

These reflections are not meant to indict. These reflections are meant to reveal. They allow us to see where intention has drifted from practice, and where small recalibrations might prevent deeper fractures. Because when values are lived, they don't need to be defended. They're simply recognized. And when they're not, no amount of messaging can hold the house together.

Structural Insights

When values are no longer lived, they begin to corrode the very culture they were meant to cultivate. Misalignment between stated values and observed behaviors is one of the most destabilizing forces within an organization. It doesn't explode overnight. Instead, it seeps in slowly through every unaddressed contradiction, every decision that prizes short-term outcomes over long-term integrity, every moment a leader fails to model what they preach.

Organizational values are not ornamental. They are not meant to be framed, recited, or laminated. Organizational values are meant to be lived. Values are, in essence, the behavioral contract between the organization and its people. When a company says "we value collaboration," employees begin to expect decision-making processes that are inclusive, feedback loops that are genuine, and team dynamics that are safe. When that same company promotes individuals who dominate rather than collaborate, or sidelines voices of dissent, it creates a disconnect that is far more than symbolic. It is systemic.

This misalignment produces a credibility gap. Employees begin to question not just the values, but the integrity of leadership itself. High-integrity, high-performing employees are often the first to notice, and the first to leave. Those who remain begin to silence themselves, disengage emotionally, or align with the organization's shadow values – the ones that are practiced but never spoken. In time, a toxic culture isn't created by bad people. It's created by good people forced to choose between survival and authenticity.

Values must be integrated into every layer of the organization's architecture. They should guide hiring decisions, shape leadership expectations, inform policy creation, influence how feedback is delivered, and determine who gets promoted. They must be defined in behavioral terms, taught explicitly, reinforced consistently, and protected vigilantly. And they must evolve as the organization evolves, but always in the open, and always in relationship to the people to whom they serve.

Cross-Tier Impact

Within the *Five Tiers Framework*, values live at the heart of **Tier 1: Foundational Core**, but their influence radiates outward into every subsequent tier. When values are misaligned at the core, the dissonance reverberates across the entire structure, distorting each tier in ways that are often subtle but deeply harmful.

In **Tier 2**, where strategy is developed, misalignment results in confusion and contradiction. Leaders may claim to prioritize innovation, but penalize failure. They may speak of transparency but make decisions behind closed doors. This breeds inconsistency in direction and erodes trust in leadership. Strategy loses its ethical compass and becomes reactive, politically driven, or disconnected from the people who carry it out.

Tier 3, where talent is developed, suffers even more acutely. Recruitment becomes a branding exercise rather than a values-aligned process. New hires quickly recognize the gap between what they were promised and what they experience. Mentorship relationships lose meaning when mentors model behaviors that contradict stated values. Succession planning becomes dangerous when promotions are based solely on performance data, rather than leadership character. Toxic leaders thrive in the absence of clear, practiced values. And once they rise, they shape cultures beneath them in their image.

Tier 4, the realm of operations, reveals misalignment through broken systems. Processes and policies that don't reflect organizational values create confusion and disengagement. A company that preaches "people first" but implements rigid policies without input sends a clear message: values are optional. Team-building initiatives feel performative. Customer service becomes mechanical. Culture becomes incoherent.

And in **Tier 5**, where continuous improvement lives, the misalignment finally reveals itself in hard data. Turnover increases. Engagement drops. Trust surveys show decline. Cultural audits reveal skepticism. But by the time the data is clear, the damage may be cultural, emotional, and systemic. Feedback loops become meaningless if they're not values-aligned. Continuous improvement without cultural integrity is little more than cosmetic renovation. It can't fix what's broken at the root.

Designing the Shift

Living your values begins with the hard work of telling the truth. Are these values real? Were they defined through inclusive dialogue or imposed from above? Do they reflect who we are at our best, or simply who we aspire to be without accountability?

Effective values are both aspirational and observable. They are shaped not just by leadership, but by actively listening to employees, partners, and communities. What do people say about the organization when no one is listening? Where does the organization shine? Where does it fall short? This process of refinement must be participatory. The goal is not perfection, but coherence.

Once values are defined or clarified, they must be translated into behaviors. Each value should be accompanied by clear expectations. If we say we value "collaboration," what does that look like in meetings, in cross-functional projects, in leadership decisions? What does "respect" mean in performance feedback or during moments of disagreement? These definitions must then be built into every system: job descriptions, interview protocols, onboarding curricula, performance evaluations, and leadership training programs.

But none of it matters if leaders do not model the values

themselves. Leadership modeling is not optional. It is the crucible where values are tested. Leaders must be trained, supported, and held accountable through mechanisms like 360-feedback, coaching, and peer reviews. They must be recognized not just for what they achieve, but for how they achieve it. And they must be willing to make decisions, especially hard ones, in alignment with core values, even when it costs them in the short term.

The greatest test of values is pressure. It is easy to act with integrity when things are calm. But during moments of conflict, crisis, or opportunity, the organization must ask: Will we stand by what we say matters most? Enduring organizations are those who answer "yes," and then prove it.

Operationalizing Change

Start by asking (not assuming) whether employees believe the organization lives its values. Use surveys, focus groups, or confidential interviews to gather honest insights. Look for where alignment is strong, and where it has fractured. Ask employees to describe the values in their own words. If they struggle, that is a data point in itself.

Conduct a "values-in-action" audit. Choose key systems such as performance reviews, hiring practices, or recent leadership decisions, and analyze whether they reflect the stated values. Identify gaps not as failures, but as invitations to realign.

Equip leaders at all levels with the tools to reinforce values consistently. This means role-playing tough decisions, exploring ethical dilemmas, learning to offer feedback through a values lens, and reflecting on their own alignment. Give them space to wrestle with the complexity because integrity is not always easy. It is earned, one decision at a time.

And finally, celebrate values-based behavior. Recognition systems should elevate those who live the values courageously, not just those who hit their numbers. Use storytelling. Share moments where values were tested and honored. Embed values into regular check-ins, team meetings, and performance conversations. Make them visible, tangible, and alive.

Executive Takeaways
Values are not ornamental, they are architectural. They are not declarations of who we wish we were, they are choices about who we are, especially when it matters most. When misaligned, values don't simply fade, they undermine the very trust and cohesion organizations depend upon. But when aligned, they become the soul of the organization. The silent agreements that shape every interaction, every decision, every culture-defining moment.

An organization can function for a while with misaligned values, especially if the results appear strong on the surface. But eventually, erosion shows – first in morale, then in performance, and finally in reputation. Rebuilding starts with returning to the truth. Who are we, really? Who do we want to be? And are we willing to do the work to close that gap?

Because the house built on sand may impress the casual observer. But it's the house built on aligned values that will stand the test of time.

Chapter 2: Leadership Checkpoints

- Do our stated values truly reflect who we are, or just who we want to be perceived as?
- Where in our organization are values consistently honored, and where are they ignored?
- Are employees able to describe and recognize our values in action?
- Have we clearly defined the behaviors that support each of our values?
- Do our policies, practices, and leadership decisions align with the values we promote?
- How are leaders held accountable when their behavior contradicts our values?
- In times of stress or change, do we protect our values, or compromise them?
- What systems of recognition or reward currently reinforce values-based behavior?
- Where might we be unintentionally rewarding behaviors that conflict with our values?
- If someone were to observe our organization in action, what values would they actually see?

TIER 2: LEADERSHIP & STRATEGY

Aligning Leaders with Organizational Structure

CHAPTER 3

THE SILO EFFECT

When Leaders Work Against Each Other

THE STORY OF JAMAL

The lodge was meant to be a reprieve, a retreat into the quiet woods, away from the relentless pulse of deadlines, bottom lines, and inboxes. The mountains stood still, wrapped in mist and pine, as if nature itself was inviting pause and reflection. The setup was perfect: catered meals, breakout rooms with oversized Post-It notes, and even a bonfire planned for the evening. The air, at least outside, felt expansive. But inside the conference room, something much tighter had already begun to form.

Jamal, the newly hired Chief Strategy Officer, took his seat quietly at the end of the long, polished table. He was new to the organization but not to the terrain of leadership. He had walked into many rooms like this one, rooms where the name tags were crisp and the smiles polite, but the undercurrents were already swirling. He hoped for alignment, or at least open dialogue. What he witnessed instead was a subtle battle for dominance cloaked in strategic language.

The Director of Programs spoke first, advocating for consolidation and focus. "We are spread too thin," she argued, "chasing too many priorities with too little coordination." She was met quickly by the Vice President of Business Development, who laid out an aggressive growth plan for entering three new markets. "We're being left behind," he said. "Expansion isn't a luxury, it's a necessity for survival." The CFO followed with warnings of budget constraints and a call for headcount reductions. "If we don't

43

tighten, we won't sustain." Then came the CHRO, whose voice softened as she emphasized employee well-being. "We can't scale on burnout," she said, pushing for increased investment in development and morale.

Each voice, on its own, made perfect sense. Each argument was backed by data, urgency, and conviction. But no one was listening. At least not beyond the point where they could prepare their own rebuttal. What should have been a strategic dialogue had become a polite turf war. Departments were no longer extensions of one mission. They had become islands, each protecting their own budgets, their own metrics, their own version of success.

As Jamal listened and took notes, he saw the symptoms clearly. Projects overlapped. Goals contradicted. Initiatives were being launched in parallel with no coordination, often undermining each other unintentionally. Roles were muddy. Accountability was diffused. Trust, though not absent, was beginning to fray. And far below the surface, the staff had already absorbed the effects. Miscommunications. Duplicated work. Exhaustion. Quiet cynicism. None of it traced back to malice. The problem wasn't bad leadership. It was fractured leadership. The problem wasn't intent. It was the result of a broken infrastructure.

On the final morning, Jamal stepped outside before the concluding session. He stood still, watching the way the fog clung to the tree line, then slowly dissolved into light. He thought about how organizations break with a slow and silent drift, not with a bang. These leaders cared. They were brilliant. But without systems to unify their direction, their brilliance was canceling itself out. And the cost wasn't just wasted effort. The cost was trust, coherence, and forward momentum.

The Strategic Lens
The lodge was a symbol – a quiet place designed for clarity – yet what Jamal encountered was emblematic of a deeper structural

misalignment that afflicts many organizations. His experience was not simply about a team in disagreement; it was a mirror into what happens when leadership loses its connective tissue. And while the symptoms were visible – duplicated efforts, internal friction, disengaged staff – the root causes were architectural. To address silos, leaders must zoom out and view their organization as a living system, not as a collection of departments. And systems either integrate or fragment depending on how intentionally they are designed.

Start by examining how leadership is defined in your organization by behavior, responsibility, and influence, not by title. Do leaders see themselves as part of a cohesive whole, or as stewards of isolated functions? When leadership identity is defined solely through departmental success, alignment will always be fragile. A collective vision must be mirrored in collective responsibility.

Then assess how strategic direction is set. Are strategies built in conversation, or in silos? Look closely at how priorities emerge. If department heads are creating goals in isolation and bringing them forward for discussion after the fact, you're likely reacting to misalignment rather than preventing it. Strategy-setting should be a shared process, not a postmortem negotiation.

Next, consider how decisions are made. Do you have clear frameworks that outline which decisions require consensus, which can be made independently, and which should be escalated? When decision rights are ambiguous, power becomes political. People start lobbying instead of collaborating. Over time, this corrodes trust and delays progress.

Incentives must also be scrutinized. If leaders are rewarded for protecting their turf rather than advancing shared outcomes, misalignment will become embedded. Metrics must reflect the full ecosystem of collaboration, cross-functional impact, and cultural contribution, not just isolated performance. The behavior you incentivize is the behavior you institutionalize.

Finally, reflect on how alignment is revisited. Strategic plans aren't static. They require regular re-engagement and reinterpretation. When was the last time your leadership team gathered to realign, not just report? And more importantly, do those sessions result in shared understanding, or just updated slides?

Jamal's moment of clarity didn't arrive in a crisis. It arrived in a quiet moment of reflection. It arrived staring into the fog, seeing the outlines of brilliance undone by lack of cohesion. This is the invitation to all organizations: to pause, to zoom out, and to ask where the conflict lives, and where the architecture failed to bring direction into harmony.

When leaders are aligned, their strategies don't cancel each other out. They compose a unified direction. And that, more than any title or tactic, is what determines whether an organization can move forward with power and purpose.

Structural Insights

Silos, contrary to popular belief, are rarely constructed through conflict. They are built quietly, over time, through a lack of structural intention. In the absence of clear integration mechanisms, leaders naturally default to optimizing for their departments. They set goals based on what they can control, defend their resources, and pursue strategies that serve their own scope. What begins as reasonable autonomy quickly calcifies into isolation.

Silos are a structural failure, not a personal one. They reflect a misalignment in how leadership roles are defined, how decisions are made, and how shared success is measured. Without intentional design, leadership becomes a collection of executives advocating for their own territories rather than collaborating toward a collective vision. In this environment, even strong leaders will pull in different directions. Not because they are adversarial, but because they are unmoored.

The danger is not just inefficiency. It's erosion. When employees see leaders contradict each other, when messaging is mixed, when projects stall due to unseen competing interests, a subtle but powerful disillusionment sets in. Frontline teams begin to disengage. Middle managers spend more time navigating interpersonal politics than implementing meaningful work. Innovation suffers from a lack of creativity and cohesion.

To prevent this, leadership must be treated as a system in motion. That system needs structure. It needs shared definitions, clarified roles, and formalized ways of aligning direction and behavior. Alignment does not happen by accident. It is cultivated. It is revisited. And it is protected.

Cross-Tier Impact

In the *Five Tiers Framework*, **Tier 2: Leadership & Strategy** translates the **Foundational Core** into unified execution. Without this tier functioning properly, the mission and values articulated in **Tier 1** remain abstract. Leadership becomes a bottleneck instead of a bridge.

When leaders are aligned in **Tier 2**, **Tier 3: Culture & People** receives clarity and consistency. Employees know what's expected. Values are not only stated, but modeled. Feedback loops work. Trust in leadership deepens because people experience continuity between words and actions.

Tier 4: Processes & Systems also benefits. Systems become coherent. Workflows are designed with cross-functional input. Teams can collaborate without stepping on each other. Resources are allocated strategically, not competitively.

And in **Tier 5: Impact & Outcomes**, the organization can finally measure what matters. Shared metrics emerge. Progress becomes transparent. Continuous improvement has a foundation to stand on because leaders are defining success in the same language. Without **Tier 2** functioning well, each of the other tiers must work harder to compensate, and the organization remains fragmented.

Designing the Shift

Building aligned leadership begins with defining what leadership is expected to be both individually and collectively. This starts with clarifying roles, not only in terms of scope and authority, but in terms of behavior and contribution to the enterprise strategy. A "Leadership Charter" can be a useful artifact, a living document that outlines shared commitments, norms, and responsibilities across the leadership team. It becomes a mirror and a map.

Strategic alignment also requires rituals, dedicated practices that ensure leaders don't just meet, but coalesce. Executive meetings should carve out time for shared reflection and enterprise-level planning. Leadership retreats should always begin with a re-grounding in the organization's mission, vision, and current state. Departmental strategies should be co-developed from overarching goals, not constructed in silos.

Decision-making must be restructured too. Clear frameworks must define what decisions require consensus, what can be made independently, and what escalation paths exist when friction arises. Without this clarity, decision-making becomes territorial and slow. Cross-functional initiatives benefit from executive sponsorship across departments, creating built-in accountability and partnership.

Incentives must be recalibrated. If leaders are rewarded solely for their department's outcomes, silos will flourish. But when collaboration, alignment, and cultural modeling are included in performance evaluations and promotion criteria, behavior changes. Leaders begin to see themselves as part of something larger. Stewards of the whole, not just guardians of their parts.

Operationalizing Change

Begin by gathering the executive team for a facilitated alignment session. Map out each department's current priorities and planned initiatives. Where do they reinforce one another? Where do they collide or duplicate? Use this mapping to surface tensions and blind spots. From there, co-create a focused set of strategic priorities for the next six to twelve months, ones that are enterprise-wide, measurable, and visible across teams.

Build a cross-functional governance structure that defines how decisions are made, how information flows, and where collaboration is expected. Assign executive sponsors to major initiatives who are accountable for outcomes and cross-functional alignment and engagement.

Introduce structured feedback mechanisms, such as 360-degree reviews, peer assessments, or organizational health surveys that evaluate collaborative behavior, not just individual performance. Use the insights to coach and support leadership growth in technical skills, and also in the art of leading together.

Tie it all back to performance development. Recognition, promotion, and advancement should reflect not only what leaders achieve, but how they lead in relationship to others. Leaders who build bridges, encourage alignment, and elevate others should be celebrated for outcomes, and for the ecosystem they help create.

Executive Takeaways

Silos do not need conflict to form. They require only a lack of shared structure. Over time, that absence becomes loud, echoing in duplicated work, disengaged employees, and fragmented execution. Leadership becomes a collection of individual ambitions rather than a coordinated system.

But alignment is possible. It begins with redefining leadership as something that happens together. It requires structure, not just style. Shared purpose, not just parallel plans. Through intentional governance, clarified roles, and aligned incentives, leadership can move from fragmentation to flow.

When leaders align, the organization breathes easier. Strategy becomes clear. Culture strengthens. Operations harmonize. And the mission, the beating heart of the work, can finally move forward. Flowing not through force, but through focused, collective momentum.

Chapter 3: Leadership Checkpoints

- How clearly defined are the roles and expectations of leaders in your organization?
- Do departmental strategies support each other, or do they exist in isolation?
- What formal practices exist to ensure regular strategic alignment among leaders?
- How is success defined at the leadership level, and does it include collaboration and cohesion?
- In what ways might existing incentive systems unintentionally reinforce siloed thinking or competition?
- How well do cross-functional teams function in your organization? Are they empowered or constrained?
- Do leaders feel ownership of enterprise-wide outcomes, or only their own departments?
- When conflict arises between departments, is there a structured path for resolution, or does tension linger?
- How often do leaders revisit the organization's vision together, not just to recite it, but to interpret it anew?
- If you asked your frontline employees how aligned leadership feels, what would they say?

CHAPTER 4

THE LEADERLESS SHIP

When No One Knows Who's In Charge

THE STORY OF DANIKA

Danika could still remember when the organization moved with rhythm and purpose. When decisions were anchored by vision, and direction was not a question, but a shared understanding. In those early years, the current was strong but steady. Projects flowed from idea to implementation, with approvals that had clear beginnings and definite ends. She had joined as a coordinator, but by the time she stepped into her current role as a middle manager, the landscape had changed dramatically. What had once felt like a well-steered vessel now felt more like a raft on open waters – everyone paddling, but no one steering.

The unraveling didn't begin with fireworks. There was no single crisis, no visible moment of fracture. Instead, it started quietly, with the sudden and unanticipated departure of the Chief Executive Officer during a significant organizational restructuring. The board, cautious and deliberate, took its time in appointing an interim. In the vacuum left behind, a peculiar shift began to occur. Senior leaders stepped forward with good intentions to fill the space, to keep things moving, to prevent panic. Yet in the absence of defined authority or agreed-upon structure, each interpreted the organization's next move differently.

What followed was subtle chaos. Leaders began to expand their reach, redrawing the map of influence without consensus. Department heads reprioritized initiatives based on personal perspectives. What once was coordinated became fragmented. Approvals vanished into thin air or emerged unexpectedly from new places. Meetings proliferated, but decisions seemed to evaporate in them. Employees, increasingly confused, began to work around the dysfunction, launching parallel projects, duplicating efforts, or simply waiting in limbo. No one wanted to make the wrong call. But no one was quite sure who could make the right one.

Danika's team, once enthusiastic and agile, grew quieter with each passing month. The problem wasn't resistance. It was disorientation. They weren't pushing back against change; they were reaching out for clarity. When Danika attempted to escalate concerns, she was told to take them to "leadership." But the definition of leadership had become mercurial. It changed depending on who you asked, what was at stake, and what day of the week it was. What once had been a cohesive system of guidance had dissolved into a patchwork of authority.

She could see it in the eyes of her colleagues. Not frustration. Not anger. Fatigue. A ship full of smart, capable people – adrift. With no single hand on the helm, and no map that everyone agreed on, the organization moved, but only in circles.

The Strategic Lens

Danika's story reveals a condition more common than many organizations care to admit: not a failure of leadership, but a failure of clarity. When no one is sure who holds the helm, or worse, when everyone believes they do, an organization begins to drift. The signs may surface slowly: hesitations around decisions, duplicated work, confused escalations, and a gradual erosion of trust in leadership. But the underlying cause is structural. A leadership system left undefined will eventually redefine itself in inconsistent, and often unproductive, ways.

To assess whether your organization is caught in a similar pattern, begin by mapping how leadership actually functions. Do so by mapping more than how it's diagrammed on paper, but how it is experienced. Who are the go-to people for decisions? Are they formally empowered, or simply the loudest or longest-tenured voices in the room? When multiple leaders are involved, are the boundaries of authority mutually understood, or negotiated on the fly? The gap between formal structure and lived reality is often where the dysfunction hides.

Examine how decisions are made and communicated. Is there a shared understanding of who approves, who informs, and who executes? Do projects regularly stall due to invisible friction or unclear ownership? If teams hesitate to move forward without explicit instruction, or if they make their own calls in the absence of direction, that's not initiative, that's improvisation born from ambiguity.

Pay close attention to how leadership transitions are handled. When someone leaves, especially someone at the top, is there a clear continuity plan, or does the organization brace for limbo? Succession gaps are one of the clearest indicators of structural fragility. Leadership should not be a role tied to a single person. Leadership should be a system that functions, even in their absence.

Also look at how leadership is socialized. Do new leaders receive a roadmap of how authority flows? Are they coached on escalation paths, cross-functional collaboration expectations, and strategic priorities? Or are they left to figure it out through osmosis and hallway conversation? Clarity in leadership must be taught as much as it is modeled.

Lastly, assess how conflict or confusion is surfaced. When questions about decision rights arise, is there a structured mechanism to resolve them? Or do they linger, whispered about but never addressed directly? An organization's ability to confront and recalibrate leadership clarity in real time is one of its strongest indicators of maturity.

Leadership is not merely about people. It is about how people are empowered, connected, and aligned within a system. Without structure, even well-meaning leaders will work at cross-purposes. The assessment, then, is not one of intention, but of design. Don't just ask who your leaders are, but whether they know how to lead together.

Structural Insights

Leadership is not simply a matter of hierarchy or titles. It is the system through which direction becomes action and vision becomes velocity. At its core, leadership structure is about the consistent flow of decision-making, responsibility, and accountability. When this flow is disrupted, or never clearly defined, organizations experience what can best be described as operational drift.

Without a clearly articulated leadership structure, decisions become bottlenecked, delayed, or duplicated. Teams expend precious energy navigating ambiguity instead of executing work. Priorities get interpreted differently by each leader, creating friction and fragmentation. Trust, even when it begins in abundance, begins to wane. And it wanes not because anyone acted maliciously, but because no one quite knew who was supposed to act at all.

This ambiguity is not the same as shared leadership or distributed decision-making. Those models require even greater clarity about who holds authority, when, and in what context. True flexibility in leadership is built on a strong foundation of defined roles and structured communication. Absent that foundation, flexibility becomes fluidity, and fluidity turns to chaos.

A well-designed leadership structure offers clarity on three core dimensions: who holds decision rights, how authority is exercised, and where accountability lives. It should define boundaries and bridges. It should tell people not only what decisions they can make, but how they escalate, delegate, and collaborate. When those structures are absent, even talented leaders will unintentionally create conflict, duplication, and confusion.

Cross-Tier Impact

Within the *Five Tiers Framework*, leadership structure is housed in **Tier 2: Leadership & Strategy**, but its influence echoes across all five tiers, including the foundational level. When authority is ambiguous, **Tier 1's** mission, vision, and values struggle to manifest in daily operations. The messaging from the top becomes inconsistent, leading employees to question which version of the truth they should follow.

In **Tier 3: Culture & People**, the impact is deeply human. Succession planning falters when no one knows how leadership is cultivated or passed on. Career development grows opaque. Employees feel disconnected from a sense of organizational progress. Mentorship, once a stronghold of institutional wisdom, loses its power when leadership itself appears unstable.

Tier 4, the home of operations and process, becomes a minefield of inefficiency. When approvals are uncertain and no one knows who owns what, delays compound. Workflows collapse. Strategic initiatives launch without coordination, or worse, they stall in silence. The team dynamic shifts from collaboration to avoidance. Most people in this situation would prefer not move forward than risk overstepping a boundary they can't see.

And in **Tier 5: Impact & Outcomes**, the damage accumulates. Feedback loops, which rely on clarity in ownership, break down. No one knows who is supposed to act on the insight, and so the organization stagnates. Continuous improvement demands responsiveness, but responsiveness requires direction. Without it, even good data leads nowhere.

Designing the Shift

To resolve leadership ambiguity, organizations must first acknowledge that the problem is structural, not personal. It's not about individual performance. It's about system design. The starting point is a comprehensive leadership audit: not just a review of the organizational chart, but a mapping of influence, decision-making flows, and authority in practice. Where do decisions originate? Where do they stall? Where are the disconnects between formal structure and lived reality?

From there, a leadership decision matrix should be developed to provide structure to every major organizational function. This matrix becomes a living document, updated as strategy evolves, but always focused on clarity. Leadership charters should accompany job descriptions, defining not just responsibilities but also the expected ways of working, communicating, and modeling values.

Orientation programs for new leaders must include more than just tactical onboarding. They must immerse leaders in the structure of decision-making, escalation paths, and cross-functional collaboration norms. And these expectations should be reinforced through consistent communication rhythms, monthly alignment meetings, weekly check-ins, and quarterly recalibrations to keep the leadership team moving in unison.

Organizational Development professionals are vital in this work. They serve as both architects and guardians of clarity, facilitating alignment sessions, monitoring system health, and prompting recalibration when clarity begins to erode. Leadership design is not a one-time event. It is an ongoing discipline.

Operationalizing Change
The path forward begins with creating intentional spaces to uncover ambiguity. Host a leadership clarity workshop with your executive and senior teams. Begin not with theory, but with scenarios. Ask: Who approves this budget? Who decides when to launch a new program? Who owns organizational culture? Capture the gaps, the contradictions, and the overlaps.

Use that insight to create your leadership map, a visible, accessible artifact that outlines decision ownership, communication pathways, and collaboration expectations. Ensure it is shared widely, not hidden in an internal folder. Everyone should be able to see the structure that guides leadership behavior.

Revisit and revise leadership job descriptions to reflect the scope of work and the manner in which authority is expected to be exercised. What behaviors reinforce alignment? What methods of communication are essential? What role does each leader play in cascading strategy and modeling culture?

Establish and normalize cross-functional leadership forums. These should not be reactive or optional. They must be rhythmic, consistent, and designed to surface misalignment early. And finally, embed accountability into the structure itself. When ambiguity arises again (and it will), the system should provide answers. Not scapegoats.

Executive Takeaways
Leadership ambiguity is a quiet force, often undetected until its effects become loud and costly. It erodes direction, dampens morale, and replaces confident action with tentative movement. But the solution does not lie in tighter control or hierarchical rigidity. It lies in intentional clarity.

A strong leadership structure gives everyone, from executives to entry-level staff, a shared understanding of who leads what, how decisions are made, and where accountability lives. It does not diminish creativity or autonomy. It enables them. With a defined helm and a collective map, the organization can once again move as one – swiftly, confidently, and in the direction that matters most.

The ship was never meant to sail without leadership. And leadership, in its truest form, was never meant to be a mystery.

Chapter 4: Leadership Checkpoints

- How clearly are leadership roles defined and communicated across your organization?
- Are employees confident in knowing who to turn to for decisions that impact their work?
- Where does leadership authority currently reside, and where does it become murky or inconsistent?
- When decisions stall, is there a system in place to identify and resolve the ambiguity, or is resolution left to chance?
- How do new leaders learn the organization's decision-making framework, and is that framework consistently reinforced over time?
- Do current leadership development efforts include a combination of tactical training and structural orientation?
- Most importantly, when leadership begins to drift – when clarity is lost – does your organization have the courage to pause and realign, or does it continue to move in circles, mistaking motion for progress?

TIER 3: CULTURE & PEOPLE

**Embedding Values in
Hiring, Retention, & Development**

CHAPTER 5

THE TOXIC WORKPLACE
When Culture Is Left To Chance

THE STORY OF MADELINE

When MeadowWave Creative first came into being, it pulsed with an energy that seemed impossible to replicate. Born from a small group of visionaries with bold ideas and little concern for hierarchy, the agency thrived in its early years on scrappiness, shared vision, and relentless creativity. Founders pulled late nights with interns, strategy meetings unfolded over pizza and whiteboards, and risk-taking was rewarded not just with applause but with laughter. There were no formalized values posted on the website, no glossy brochures filled with lofty ideals. But everyone felt it. The culture was unmistakable. It was free, bold, collaborative, a little chaotic, and deeply human.

As the agency grew, so did its ambitions. Larger clients came knocking, demanding more process, more sophistication, and more polish. The leadership team expanded, bringing in executives with industry experience, and new offices dotted the map in cities that once seemed out of reach. But along with that success came a shift, one that was as gradual as it was insidious. The culture began to unravel, not in dramatic clashes, but in subtle, accumulating tension. Gossip became more frequent. Managers operated with vastly different expectations. Talent left as quietly as it arrived, often after only a few months. People still smiled in meetings, still posted team lunches on Slack, but the spark was dimming.

When Madeline stepped into her role as Head of People and Culture, she was tasked with answering a deceptively simple question: "What happened?" She didn't begin with solutions. She began with stories, listening sessions with employees across every level and department. What emerged was not anger, but fatigue.

Team members felt unseen. New rules clashed with old instincts. Every manager seemed to play by a different set of rules. There was no longer a shared understanding of how to behave, collaborate, or even disagree. One designer, voice trembling with equal parts hope and resignation, put it plainly: "It's like we're all trying to be part of something meaningful, but no one will tell us what 'it' is anymore."

Madeline understood the core of the problem. Culture had been treated as something innate and unspoken, rather than something to be named, reinforced, and protected. What MeadowWave had mistaken for freedom had long since become confusion. What once felt organic now felt rudderless. There were still kombucha taps and bean bag chairs, but without structure, those trappings had become ornamental, not meaningful. The agency wasn't suffering from a lack of perks. It was suffering from a lack of cultural scaffolding.

The Strategic Lens

MeadowWave's decline wasn't the result of malice, incompetence, or a single explosive event. It was a slow disintegration of cohesion. So quiet it almost escaped notice. And that's what makes cultural drift so dangerous: it doesn't announce itself. It settles in. Unnoticed, unchallenged, and over time, normalized.

To assess whether a similar erosion is taking place in your organization, begin by examining not what your values say, but how your people experience them. Culture is not tested when things are calm. It's tested in conflict, in ambiguity, in moments of growth or pressure. When policies change, when leadership turns over, when priorities shift, do your values serve as a compass, or do they disappear from the conversation altogether?

Step back and ask: Do employees across the organization have a shared understanding of how people are expected to show up? Are there unwritten rules that carry more weight than the stated values? If people feel they must choose between fitting in and being authentic, your culture may be running on performance, not trust.

Look also at the behavior of managers and leaders. Are they cultural multipliers or contradictions? Do they model the values they speak to? And when they don't, is there a mechanism for addressing that misalignment? Many organizations claim to care about culture, but avoid the discomfort of naming and correcting the behaviors that actively corrode it. That silence is not neutral. That silence is consent.

Assess how culture is integrated into your systems. Are hiring and promotions values-informed, or purely results-based? Do feedback mechanisms allow for honesty about interpersonal dynamics, psychological safety, and trust? Or are they narrowly focused on productivity and output? An organization that fails to include cultural health in its performance metrics is choosing short-term deliverables over long-term viability.

And perhaps most importantly, pay attention to the spaces between your systems – those informal conversations, Slack threads, hallway glances. What is being tolerated? What is being avoided? What truths are being whispered, but never spoken aloud? Culture is often clearest in what goes unsaid.

When culture is left to chance, it eventually calcifies into something that resists reflection. But when examined with care, and recalibrated with intention, it becomes one of the most powerful forces of alignment and resilience an organization can cultivate. The assessment is not about judgment. It's about recognition. Because we cannot strengthen what we refuse to name.

Structural Insights
Culture, at its essence, is not a brand story or a carefully curated vibe. Culture is the lived reality of the workplace. It is embedded in how people treat one another, how decisions are made, how

conflict is handled, and how success is defined. It shows up in tone, timing, behavior, and consequence. Culture is not what's written in a mission statement. It's what's tolerated in a meeting. It's not what leaders say during onboarding. It's what they do during times of stress.

Many organizations make the mistake of romanticizing culture as something that just "happens." In the beginning, it often does. Founders bring values to life through their behavior, and early teams adopt norms by watching and mimicking. But over time, as organizations scale, the myth of an "organic culture" begins to fray. Without intentional stewardship, culture begins to drift, becoming increasingly dependent on personalities rather than principles. When no one owns culture, no one protects it. And that's when dysfunction starts to fester.

Toxic culture rarely announces itself with drama. Instead, it creeps in through minor inconsistencies. A manager shows favoritism. A high performer gets away with bullying behavior. A team begins to communicate through sarcasm and avoidance. Small lapses go unchecked until they become norms. Employees stop speaking up, not out of fear, but because they no longer believe their voice matters. Trust erodes. Initiative declines. Psychological safety disappears. And still, the company may continue to hit its targets. Until one day ... it doesn't.

A sustainable culture requires structure. It requires values that are articulated and embedded into how the organization hires, evaluates, promotes, and responds. It demands systems that reward cultural alignment and call out behaviors that break it. Culture doesn't just survive in rituals and posters. It survives in accountability, consistency, and feedback.

Cross-Tier Impact
Tier 3: Culture & People of the *Five Tiers Framework* is often where the organization's soul either flourishes or withers. But its

health is entirely dependent on the strength of **Tier 1** and **Tier 2**. When the foundational tier lacks clarity around mission, vision, and values, culture becomes a guessing game. Employees try to do the right thing, but they don't know what "right" looks like. The organization's purpose becomes abstract, and people begin to create their own definitions of success.

If leadership in **Tier 2** is misaligned or contradictory, culture becomes fractured. Employees pay attention to what leaders say and more accurately, what they do. More importantly, employees pay attention to whether those actions support or betray the stated values. If leaders make decisions that reward speed over respect, or profit over integrity, the message is loud and clear: culture is conditional. Leadership behavior is the most powerful signal in any organization. Without alignment at the top, culture cannot stabilize below.

In **Tier 4**, operations either reinforce or erode culture. Toxic cultures often suffer from convoluted processes, passive-aggressive communication, and conflicting expectations. People operate in silos, guard their turf, and struggle to collaborate. By contrast, healthy cultures streamline work because values provide a shared language and shared standard for execution.

And **Tier 5**, the realm of continuous improvement, relies entirely on cultural health. Feedback cannot be successful in an environment where people are afraid of judgment or punishment. Innovation requires vulnerability. Growth requires reflection. When culture is toxic, none of that is possible. People protect themselves instead of contributing.

Culture is not an initiative. It is the invisible system that either connects or divides every tier of the organization.

Designing the Shift
The path to a healthy culture begins with definition, but defi-

nition alone is not enough. Culture must be operationalized, translated into specific, observable behaviors that everyone can understand and practice. This work should be participatory. Culture is not created in an executive retreat. It is uncovered in conversations with employees, with teams, with those who know the pulse of the organization from the inside.

Once values are defined in action terms, they must be embedded into every system that touches people: hiring rubrics, interview questions, onboarding checklists, performance reviews, coaching frameworks, and promotion criteria. This ensures that culture is not just aspirational, but structural. New employees should encounter the culture from day one beyond slogans, and through mentorship, storytelling, and modeled behavior.

Leadership development must go beyond skill training. Leaders must be equipped to model culture, coach to it, and protect it. This means teaching leaders how to deliver feedback through a values lens, how to handle conflict with integrity, and how to lead with consistency. It also means holding leaders accountable when their behavior violates the very values they are expected to uphold.

There must also be clear, safe mechanisms for surfacing cultural concerns. Culture cannot be healthy if the only feedback is praise. Anonymous surveys, confidential reporting tools, open forums, and protected dialogue sessions are not "extras." They are essential safeguards. When feedback is surfaced, the organization must act on it visibly. Culture cannot be performative. It must be responsive.

Operationalizing Change
Start by listening. Ask your people when the culture has felt strongest. Ask when it felt weakest. Ask what behaviors they associate with your stated values, and what behaviors they see that contradict them. Look for patterns across departments, demographics, and tenures. This is not just data collection. It's truth-telling.

Use this insight to develop a cultural blueprint, a values-to-behavior guide that names what each value looks like in real-world terms. Make it a reference point, not a branding piece. Use it in meetings, reviews, and hiring panels. Embed it into the daily life of the organization.

Redesign onboarding to prioritize cultural immersion. Match new hires with culture carriers. Share stories that illuminate your values in action. Review their experience after 30-, 60-, and 90-days (even up to 365 days) for task alignment and cultural connection.

Revamp your performance management system to reflect your values. Recognize and reward employees who model cultural behaviors. Coach those who drift from them. Evaluate leaders not just on what they achieve, but how they achieve it.

Establish cultural rituals that keep values visible: weekly reflections, values-based recognitions, storytelling at town halls, and monthly "culture check-ins." Make culture a rhythm, not a relic.

Executive Takeaways

Culture is not what you say about your organization, it's how your organization feels when people walk through the door. When left to chance, culture unravels slowly, quietly, and dangerously. But with intention, culture becomes an essential force of cohesion, trust, and energy.

A healthy culture is not soft. It is rigorous. It is defined, practiced, protected, and measured. It is a living system that requires leadership, structure, and rhythm. It cannot be outsourced to Human Resources or contained in a poster. It must be lived.

When culture is aligned with values, embedded into systems, and stewarded by leaders, it becomes your greatest asset. Not because it's perfect, but because it's real. And real culture is what allows people to do their best work, together.

Chapter 5: Leadership Checkpoints

- Do the values of your organization translate into daily behavior, or are they limited to messaging?
- Where do employees experience inconsistencies or cultural drift, and how do they make sense of those moments?
- What systems are in place to surface cultural concerns, and are they trusted?
- In your hiring, evaluation, and leadership development processes, are values integrated into decision-making and reinforcement?
- What behaviors are being rewarded in your organization, and do they truly reflect the culture you want to build?

CHAPTER 6

THE GHOST OF LEADERSHIP PAST

When Organizations Struggle With Change

.

THE STORY OF BRAYLON

Braylon had always been the kind of leader who looked toward the horizon. Sharp, strategic, and curious by nature, he joined the regional health agency with a belief in its mission and a hope that fresh ideas would be welcomed. But what he found was something different, an invisible weight pressing against every proposal he made, a kind of organizational gravity that pulled innovation back to the ground before it could lift off.

The agency was known for its stability. It had weathered leadership changes, political cycles, and funding shifts with a quiet resilience. But that resilience had hardened into resistance. Leadership hadn't changed in decades, at least not in spirit. Titles shifted, people retired, but the way things were done stayed the same. It was a place where systems were inherited, not questioned. Where the past wasn't just remembered, it was enforced.

Braylon's first attempt to reimagine the intake process was met with skepticism cloaked in politeness. "That's interesting," someone offered. "But we've found what we have works just fine." A month later, his pilot program was shelved. Not with objection, but with delay. "We'll revisit next quarter." But next quarter never came.

He started noticing how new hires were quietly nudged into conformity. How promising voices went quiet in meetings. How legacy leaders – those who'd built the place from the ground up – spoke of change as something that would come *someday*, as if time alone would modernize them.

The final sign came when a talented program coordinator, only six months in, submitted her resignation. "I don't want to fight a ghost," she told Braylon during her exit interview. "Everyone's still working for the leaders who left years ago. Or maybe they never really left."

Braylon stared at her empty chair after she left. He understood what she meant. The organization was haunted. Not by malice, but by memory. By systems and norms so embedded they'd become invisible. And unless something changed, the next wave of leaders would never have the space to lead.

The Strategic Lens

Braylon's story is not just about change being blocked, it's about the quieter, deeper grip of tradition left unexamined. For many organizations, it's not resistance in the form of refusal that undermines progress, but resistance cloaked in reverence. To assess whether your organization is haunted by its own legacy, you must widen the lens beyond surface behaviors or isolated decisions, and look at the full scaffolding of structure, story, and symbolism.

Begin with the unwritten norms. What assumptions go unchallenged in meetings? Are new ideas welcomed, or quietly absorbed and dissolved? If people routinely preface innovation with disclaimers like, "I know this might not be how we've done things…," that's a signal. Not just of fear, but of reverence out of balance. Identify where historical practices are considered default, not because they are still effective, but because they are still familiar.

Examine where decisions are made and by whom. Do certain individuals or departments wield informal authority disproportionate to their formal roles? Are projects quietly routed through legacy power channels? Organizational ghosts often linger in decision pathways, where previous influence was never sunset, only softened.

Take a close look at the way leadership roles are structured and transferred. Are new leaders shaped by the future needs of the organization, or are they subtly pressured to replicate the style and sensibilities of those who came before? If succession is treated more as ceremonial continuity than strategic renewal, the organization is prioritizing comfort over relevance.

Evaluate how legacy is treated in conversation. Are traditions openly discussed, interrogated, and evolved, or are they only celebrated? Is historical knowledge a source of wisdom or an unspoken directive? If innovation requires navigating a maze of "used to be" rather than a map of "what's next," then legacy has ceased to serve.

Finally, listen to the organizational language around time. Are people waiting for permission to lead? Waiting for the old guard to retire? Waiting for next quarter, next year, next hire to "finally" do something differently? When hope is always projected forward but never activated, it's not planning. That approach creates paralysis.

The purpose of this assessment is not to erase the past. It is to illuminate how the past is currently shaping the present, and whether that influence is still earning its place. Some legacies deserve to be passed on. Others deserve to be thanked, then released.

Real change requires clear eyes, steady hands, and the courage to ask: Are we building a future, or protecting a memory?

Structural Insights

Resistance to change isn't always loud. It doesn't always arrive as a hard "no." Sometimes it shows up as hesitation, as delay, as endless "revisiting" of ideas that threaten the familiar. In organizations with long-standing leaders or deeply rooted traditions, the resistance often hides behind phrases like "this is how we've always done it," or "we tried that once."

While legacy leadership provides continuity, context, and institutional memory, it becomes problematic when it begins to reject adaptation. Structures, policies, and leadership pathways that once served the organization well, may now constrain it. And without deliberate structural evolution, the organization becomes unwelcoming to new ideas, new talent, and new direction.

Outdated job descriptions, ambiguous roles, informal power hierarchies, and hiring practices that favor cultural sameness over future readiness are all signs of a structure in stasis. Innovation becomes isolated. Onboarding becomes assimilation. And succession planning becomes ceremonial, if it exists at all.

The issue is not the existence of legacy. It's the absence of reflection. Organizational Development professionals must create space for honoring the past while dismantling what no longer serves. This is not just cultural, it's structural. It requires a reshaping of leadership expectations, redesigning development systems, and introducing governance that invites change rather than creating delays in it.

Cross-Tier Impact

In the *Five Tiers Framework*, this chapter is rooted in **Tier 3: Culture & People**, but its shadow reaches across all five tiers.

In **Tier 1**, legacy systems cloud the mission. A vision that once inspired now feels outdated. Core values may still be relevant, but without reexamination, they risk becoming relics instead of future organizational drivers.

Tier 2 is compromised when leadership roles are occupied by those more committed to the past than to the future. Strategic alignment gives way to personal legacy preservation. Leadership development becomes exclusive, focused only on reinforcing what's already in existence.

Tier 4 suffers in silence. Operational systems become convoluted, with unnecessary complexity born from outdated processes. Technology upgrades are rejected. Interdepartmental communication defaults to ritual over efficiency.

And in **Tier 5**, feedback loops fail. Improvement becomes symbolic. Change efforts are introduced with flair but quietly withdrawn when they challenge legacy norms. The organization performs the choreography of innovation but never actually moves.

Integration requires courage. It asks leaders to become stewards of evolution, not just protectors of tradition.

Designing the Shift

Transformation, at its most honest and enduring, does not begin with a formal rollout or a new slogan emblazoned across an intranet banner. It begins in conversation, in the quiet courage of sitting with the past and asking what parts of it still serve. Not all legacies are burdens, but even the most storied traditions need to be examined in the light of current purpose. Organizational Development professionals are uniquely positioned to facilitate this shift by creating environments where reverence and reflection can coexist.

Legacy Reflection Sessions should be thoughtfully designed, not as critique forums, but as intergenerational bridges. These sessions are most powerful when long-tenured leaders are invited into a shared inquiry, not asked to defend the systems they once helped build. The key question is not "What should we keep?" (which tends to invite defensiveness), but rather "What have we outgrown?" This reframing opens the door to honoring what was, while allowing room for what must now take shape. These conversations must be guided with empathy, humility, and psychological safety. They require facilitators who understand both the emotional gravity of letting go and the organizational necessity of moving forward.

Following these dialogues, a Structural Health Scan offers a diagnostic view of where legacy is holding firm and where it may be holding back. This is a comprehensive evaluation of formal structures and informal systems: roles that no longer reflect reality, workflows that have become unnecessarily convoluted, policies that contradict the organization's stated values, and development practices that favor familiarity over future readiness. The goal is not simply to clean house, but to create clarity. To make visible the parts of the system that have become invisible through habit.

From here, the work shifts toward designing what comes next. Future Leadership Profiles become essential blueprints, not for who a leader is, but for what the organization needs them to become. These profiles should reflect the competencies required to navigate uncertainty, inspire diverse teams, and drive innovation while remaining anchored in the organization's mission. These are not aspirational templates that sit in binders; they are living guides that inform recruitment, influence the structure of development programs, and serve as a benchmark for succession planning.

Equally vital is embedding mentorship in multiple directions. Traditional models of passing down wisdom are no longer sufficient in a world where change accelerates by the day. Reverse mentorship programs create a reciprocal dynamic, where emerging leaders provide insight, context, and digital fluency to senior leaders. This shared vulnerability encourages humility, flattens power hierarchies, and brings a fresh lens to systems that may have gone unquestioned for too long.

Over time, organizations must commit to an intentional rhythm for rotating responsibilities, introducing new voices, and inviting continuous perspective shifts. Renewal doesn't mean erasure. It means building elasticity into the system so no one leader becomes irreplaceable, and no one vision becomes too dominant to be challenged. This also allows emerging leaders to gain exposure, experience, and the opportunity to influence without needing to wait for a vacancy.

Most importantly, every structural change must remain tethered to the deeper truth: mission and service. The goal is not to dismantle for the sake of movement. It is to build a structure that reflects who the organization is becoming, not just who it once was. Change that loses sight of purpose becomes disorienting. Change that honors purpose becomes transformative.

Operationalizing Change

Begin by organizing a Legacy Systems Audit. This is not a surface-level review. It is a courageous deep dive into the organizational architecture. Form a team composed of members across generations, tenures, and departments. Give them the task of identifying outdated systems, norms, workflows, and cultural rituals that no longer serve the current reality. Assign each artifact a score that reflects two core questions: How much risk does this pose to the organization's future? And how well does this still align with our strategic direction? This exercise creates a shared map of what needs to be preserved, reimagined, or released.

Next, facilitate a Cross-Generational Leadership Dialogue. This gathering is a structured conversation between veteran leaders who carry institutional memory and newer employees who bring fresh eyes and new energy. The objective is not debate, but discovery. Ask them to share stories, moments when the organization felt most alive, most innovative, most aligned. Ask them to name moments when the past felt like a weight instead of a guide. In the overlap of these stories, patterns emerge: shared values that transcend time, and also tensions that must be addressed head-on.

With those insights in hand, revise job descriptions and leadership charters across the board. Strip them of legacy language that speaks only to maintenance, and rewrite them with clarity, courage, and commitment to future impact. A job description should no longer be a static list of tasks. It should be a narrative of purpose, behavior, and contribution. Leadership charters should name how power is shared, how communication is expected to flow, and how accountability is defined in both upward and downward directions.

Simultaneously, design and launch a Succession Activation Map. This is more than a list of potential replacements. It is a dynamic plan that names roles vulnerable to stagnation, identifies developmental gaps in readiness pipelines, and outlines clear, time-bound strategies for mentoring, cross-training, and exposure. The map should be reviewed quarterly and include measurable outcomes, such as readiness scores and leadership mobility metrics.

To unite all of these efforts, publish a Collective Future Statement. This should not be drafted solely by the executive team. Instead, open the process to the full organization. Host workshops. Use anonymous prompts.

Ask questions like: What are we proud of? What do we want to be known for in five years? What should we carry forward, and what must we leave behind?

The resulting statement should serve as a compass. A symbol of shared ownership and forward momentum. Display it. Celebrate it. Use it to guide decisions, behaviors, and investments.

Executive Takeaways
Organizations do not resist change out of ignorance or stubbornness alone. More often, it is reverence that keeps them still. Reverence for those who came before. Reverence for systems that once served well. Reverence for familiar rhythms that create comfort. But reverence, when left unexamined, becomes rigidity. It builds walls where there should be windows. It guards old scaffolding long after the building has outgrown it.

The ghost of leadership past is not always a person. It is just as often a forgotten workflow, a fear of offending tradition, or a hidden belief that innovation is somehow disrespectful to legacy. But individuals across all levels have the tools to invite these ghosts into the light. Not to banish them. But to understand them, thank them, and move forward with clarity and compassion.

Because change is not inherently a break. It is a bridge. And when that bridge is built with care, when it honors the stones beneath it but reaches confidently across the divide, it becomes the very thing that reconnects an organization with its deeper purpose. Not as it was imagined decades ago. But as it must become now.

Chapter 6: Leadership Checkpoints

- What systems, behaviors, or leadership practices are no longer aligned with your current strategy?
- How does reverence for tradition show up in your organization? Is it helpful or is it limiting?
- Do employees have space to challenge outdated norms without risk?
- Are legacy leaders invited to mentor and evolve or expected to defend and maintain?
- What could your organization become if legacy were used as a launchpad, not a leash?

TIER 4:
PROCESSES
& SYSTEMS

Creating Operational Efficiency

CHAPTER 7

THE MAZE

When Process Overcomplicates Progress

THE STORY OF AMINA

By the time Amina reached the fifth step in submitting what should have been a simple supply request, she was already drafting her resignation in her head. She wasn't new to complexity, as her background in systems thinking had prepared her for tangled workflows and interdependencies, but nothing could have prepared her for the procedural labyrinth she encountered at the municipal housing agency.

She had joined with optimism. Amina believed deeply in the agency's mission to improve housing access, and she hoped to bring operational insight that could streamline processes for the overworked staff and underserved community. But her first week felt like entering a time capsule sealed in layers of bureaucracy. To request a printer, she was instructed to locate Form 37-B, get it signed by two separate managers, scan and upload it into an outdated database, and then wait three weeks for budget review. By the end of that journey, her team had either found a workaround or given up altogether.

The rest of her onboarding wasn't much better. Training materials were scattered across inconsistent systems. Some were outdated; others were duplicated. Institutional knowledge had no formal home. It was stored in the heads of long-tenured employees like Rhonda, who knew the backdoor pathways to systems but was, unfortunately, on leave during Amina's onboarding. "Just ask Rhonda" had become the agency's unofficial operating principle.

But this wasn't just about office supplies or login access. Every process, whether for project approvals, staffing requests, budgeting, or communication, was riddled with unnecessary checkpoints. No one seemed able to trace why these steps existed. Layers of process had accumulated over time, each added in response to a specific issue, audit, or leadership preference. No one had taken the time to clear the underbrush. The result was a sprawling procedural jungle. An organization built on systems designed by people who never had to walk through them.

Employees weren't exhausted from the mission. They were exhausted from navigating it. Innovation was quietly discouraged by layers of approvals. Momentum was killed not by resistance to change, but by the sheer effort required to make it.

Amina didn't want to start a revolution. She simply wanted her team to do their work without being strangled by the systems meant to support them. But every suggestion to streamline was met with vague warnings about compliance or the dreaded refrain: "That's just how we've always done it." In this agency, bureaucracy wasn't just a structure. It had become the culture. And it was winning.

The Strategic Lens

Amina's experience highlights a truth many organizations are reluctant to face: complexity is not always a sign of sophistication. Sometimes, it's a sign of neglect. To assess whether your organization's systems have drifted from support to obstruction, you must take a systemic view, not just of individual processes, but of the mindset and history that created them.

Start by examining the organization's philosophy of process. Are workflows designed to empower, or to prevent? Is the default mindset one of trust or control? If most systems were built in response to fear – of mistakes, audits, or bad actors – they likely reflect overcompensation, not optimization. Complexity born from caution may feel safe, but it slowly erodes initiative.

Next, look at the invisible architecture, the layers of work-around and informal "know how" that keep the wheels turning. Who are the "go-to" people like Rhonda? If systems rely heavily on individual memory rather than institutional documentation, the organization is not scalable, it's fragile. Legacy knowledge is valuable, but when it becomes a substitute for clarity, it traps innovation in a bottleneck of personalities.

Assess where time is being lost without value returned. Identify your high-friction zones: purchasing, approvals, onboarding, reporting. If employees must repeatedly explain, follow up, or "just check" with someone to get things moving, you are witnessing structural drag. Track how long tasks take, how many people are touched in the process, and whether each touch adds clarity, quality, or just delay.

Consider the feedback loop health. Do people feel safe naming inefficiencies? Are there mechanisms to suggest and test improvements, or is improvement permission-based and top-down? If innovation requires going through the very bureaucracy that stifles it, most people will choose silence over struggle. The absence of complaints is not evidence of contentment. It's often evidence of fatigue.

Lastly, evaluate the alignment between process and purpose. Can each step in a workflow be tied back to a strategic value or operational necessity? Or have policies accumulated like sediment, layered over time without ever being cleared? When no one remembers why a rule exists, that rule becomes a weight, not a safeguard.

This assessment is not about burning it all down. It's about untangling the overgrowth and replanting only what's necessary. Efficient systems are not shallow, they are intentional. And in a healthy organization, process doesn't feel like a maze. It feels like a map.

Structural Insights

Processes are the lifeblood of any organization. They are the conduits through which decisions, resources, and action flow. When functioning well, processes enable consistency, clarity, and efficiency. But when they become overly complex, outdated, or layered with unnecessary approvals, they begin to choke the very operations they are meant to facilitate.

The mistake many organizations make is equating more steps with more control. Every new policy, every added layer of approval, often stems from a well-intentioned desire to minimize risk or ensure oversight. But without intentional design and periodic review, these additions become burdensome. What starts as a single protective measure becomes part of a convoluted system that no longer reflects the size, speed, or purpose of the organization.

These process inefficiencies often originate from a few core issues: outdated technologies that haven't scaled with organizational needs, overlapping responsibilities that create confusion, lack of documentation that leads to reliance on individual memory, and a fear-based culture where holding authority over decisions is perceived as power. Compliance becomes weaponized, and decision-making becomes risk-averse. In such environments, time is no longer a resource. It becomes a toll.

Eventually, the cost is more than just time. Employee morale erodes when daily workflows feel punitive or purposeless. High-potential staff leave not because they lack passion, but because they cannot spend their careers untangling knots. Innovation stalls because trying something new means navigating a minefield of outdated protocols. The organization may still be moving, but it's doing so slowly, inefficiently, and with growing frustration from those tasked with keeping it going.

Cross-Tier Impact

This chapter sits squarely in **Tier 4: Processes & Systems** of the *Five Tiers Framework*, but its influence reaches across the entire structure. Without clarity of mission and values from **Tier 1**, processes drift toward control rather than purpose. Policies begin to reflect fear instead of trust, and decision-making becomes more about avoiding mistakes than creating value.

Tier 2 suffers when leaders fail to challenge the processes they inherit. When leadership is disconnected from day-to-day operations, inefficiencies are overlooked or accepted as "just the way it is." Without alignment at the top, broken systems persist because no one is incentivized, or empowered, to fix them.

Tier 3: Culture & People takes a direct hit. Overengineered processes demoralize staff. New hires find themselves confused or disengaged, and seasoned employees operate in a constant state of workaround. Growth and development plans stall, not because of individual limitations, but because the systems don't allow for forward movement.

Even **Tier 5: Impact & Outcomes** falters in the face of procedural overload. When giving feedback requires filling out a form that leads nowhere, employees stop trying. When innovation means a six-month approval process, new ideas die quietly. The feedback loop closes not with insight, but with silence.

True operational excellence doesn't exist in isolation. It's a critical hinge point that either propels the organization forward or traps it in endless motion without progress.

Designing the Shift
The path to operational clarity begins with transparency. Organizations must map out their existing processes to understand where friction lives. This requires bringing together people from across departments to walk through workflows step-by-step. The goal is not to assign blame, but to illuminate where time, effort, and clarity are being lost.

Once the current state is documented, organizations must shift their thinking from "control" to "value." Every step in a process should serve a purpose in supporting outcomes, protecting essential risk, or enhancing service. Redundancies, unnecessary approvals, or steps that exist "just because" should be identified for redesign or removal.

This redesign should follow principles rooted in simplicity and adaptability. Workflows should prioritize the end user, whether that's an employee trying to get supplies or a manager submitting a budget. Oversight should be right-sized: enough to ensure accountability, not so much that it stifles initiative. Policies should be built on guiding principles rather than exhaustive procedures. The goal is not to eliminate structure, but to make it supportive, not oppressive.

Leadership must model and reinforce this shift. Process improvement should not be a side project. It should be a core part of leadership accountability. Leaders must be trained to champion simplification and actively seek input from those who use the systems most. Recognition should go to teams that find efficiencies, reduce bottlenecks, or bring forward solutions.

Operationalizing Change
The first practical step is conducting a full Process Health Check. Identify one or two high-frustration workflows and follow them from start to finish. Who's involved? How long does it take? Where does it stall? Document every layer.

Next, bring cross-functional teams together in a Systems Alignment Workshop. Encourage open dialogue about how processes intersect, where duplication occurs, and where communication breaks down. These workshops should feel like design sessions, not complaint forums, where the goal is to build smarter, not just vent louder.

Once pain points are identified, implement a small pilot project. Streamline one process, perhaps onboarding or reporting, and test it with a limited group. Monitor impact on time, morale, and outcomes. Use those results to inform larger changes.

To support broader ownership, you can create a Decision Rights Matrix. Clarify who can approve what, where autonomy can be exercised, and when escalation is actually necessary. This empowers employees at every level to act within clear boundaries, reducing unnecessary delay.

Finally, build continuous feedback into process management. Ask regularly, "Was this useful? Efficient? Clear?" Make it easy to suggest improvements. Review these suggestions as part of a regular operations review cycle. Improvement must be constant, not crisis-driven.

Executive Takeaways

An organization should not feel like a maze to the people who power it.

When systems become tangled in complexity and tradition, the organization begins to suffocate under its own weight. What once felt like thoughtful diligence becomes a culture of delay and disempowerment. But it doesn't have to stay that way. Through transparency, accountability, and a return to purpose, processes can once again become tools, not traps.

Operational excellence isn't about moving fast. It's about moving clearly. With the right structural changes, the maze becomes a map. And everyone can move forward with confidence.

Chapter 7: Leadership Checkpoints

- Where do employees spend the most time fighting the system instead of working within it?
- How do your current workflows reflect your values or contradict them?
- Who owns process improvement in your organization? Is it a shared responsibility?
- Do employees have the autonomy to bypass or improve inefficient steps, or are they bound by rigidity?
- If you redesigned one process this quarter, what impact could it have?

CHAPTER 8

THE ILLUSION OF STRUCTURE

When Invisible Gaps Disrupt Everyday Work

THE STORY OF JORDAN

On his second week at Clearwater Health Services, Jordan found a dusty binder labeled *2011 Employee Handbook* wedged between a coffeemaker and an unplugged fax machine in the breakroom. He opened it out of curiosity. By the third page, he realized something startling. Not a single policy had been updated in over a decade. Entire sections referenced systems that had since been retired, managers who had long since left, and protocols that no one currently followed.

Yet when he asked around about onboarding processes, dispute resolution, or even PTO requests, people gestured vaguely toward that same outdated document. They'd reply, "It's in the handbook, I think," or, "I just ask Linda. She's been here forever." Linda, it turned out, had recently retired. And with her went the last living memory of how certain things were done.

Jordan wasn't surprised by the gaps. He was surprised by how little anyone acknowledged them. On the surface, Clearwater appeared to be functioning. Teams met their deliverables. Compliance reports got filed. But beneath that functionality was a network of improvisation. People created their own checklists, made assumptions about authority, rerouted forms through informal channels, and relied heavily on who they knew to get things done.

There were no written escalation paths. No shared repository for procedural updates. No consistent language between departments. A frontline supervisor once emailed Jordan to ask, "Can I approve shift swaps?" followed by, "Or do I need to run that by Payroll? HR? My Director? I can't find it anywhere." He wasn't alone. Managers across departments admitted they avoided certain decisions entirely for fear of stepping outside some invisible rule they didn't know existed.

The deeper Jordan looked, the more he realized this wasn't a problem of broken systems. It was a problem of absent ones. Clearwater didn't need process improvement. It needed process definition.

So he began charting what wasn't there. He started with workflow mapping sessions, inviting staff to explain how things "actually" got done. Sticky notes filled conference room walls: "We just call Maria," "This form disappears for 3 days," "Nobody knows who signs off on this." Jordan listened, documented, and cross-referenced every workaround, every ad hoc decision, every moment where guesswork stood in for guidance.

What emerged wasn't dysfunction. It was adaptation. People weren't failing the system. They were building it in real time.

But even ingenuity has its limits. Without shared structure, no one could scale their solutions. No one could trust their choices. And no one could lead with clarity, because no one could see the whole map.

That was the real crisis. Not chaos, but invisibility.

The Strategic Lens
Jordan's experience surfaces a systemic reality present in many organizations: not all breakdowns come from dysfunction. Some come from absence. When processes aren't intentionally designed, they default to habit, memory, or improvisation. What emerges is not a system but a patchwork. Each leader, manager, or employee fills in the blanks differently, based on what they assume, remember, or invent.

To assess whether your organization is operating within a clear and functional system, or simply pretending one exists, begin by examining the visibility of workflows. Ask yourself: Can employees at any level describe, with consistency, how key processes work? If the answers vary by department, tenure, or role, you may be managing through myth rather than structure.

Next, evaluate documentation. Are handbooks, SOPs, and onboarding materials current, accessible, and reflective of reality? Outdated documents don't just cause confusion. They erode credibility. When employees discover that written guidance conflicts with how things actually operate, trust in leadership and systems declines. Instead of turning to policy, people begin turning to people selectively, informally, and inconsistently.

Pay close attention to where decisions stall. When no one is quite sure who owns a process or what the next step is, progress becomes dependent on personalities rather than structure. This ambiguity creates friction, workarounds, and burnout. The system becomes invisible not because it doesn't exist, but because it doesn't work.

Finally, observe the consequences of absence. Where no process lives, improvisation thrives. And while autonomy can be powerful, unsupervised improvisation across critical workflows leads to duplicated efforts, missed steps, or inconsistent service delivery. Over time, what looks like agility reveals itself as drift.

Invisibility is rarely intentional, but it's always costly. Systems that aren't clarified become systems that are quietly rewritten by every person who interacts with them. And without intervention, that fragmentation becomes the norm.

Structural Insights

A broken system is obvious. But an invisible one? That's far more dangerous. When processes don't exist, aren't documented, or are so outdated they no longer reflect reality, organizations begin to function on institutional memory, gut instinct, and whispered advice. That might work for a time, especially when teams are stable and experienced. But as people shift, roles evolve, and expectations increase, the absence of operational clarity becomes a source of confusion, inconsistency, and quiet failure.

Tier 4: Processes & Systems is not just about efficiency. It is the scaffolding that holds organizational intentions in place. Without defined workflows, systems become reactive. Leaders are forced to make ad hoc decisions without reference points. Staff create workarounds that may solve the immediate issue but introduce long-term risk. These short-term solutions accumulate until no one knows where the real path begins, or who laid it in the first place.

The absence of process breeds dependency on people, not structure. Instead of asking, "What does the system say?" employees begin to ask, "Who do I ask?" And that question, repeated across enough scenarios, creates internal inequity. Knowledge becomes concentrated. Access becomes personal. Outcomes become unpredictable.

Furthermore, ambiguity in systems often hides deeper structural fractures. Policies may exist but are inconsistently applied. Roles may be titled, but their responsibilities overlap or remain unclear. Technology might be in place but misaligned with actual workflow needs. The result is duplication, delay, and disengagement.

And when employees stop trusting the system, they stop investing in it. They disengage, not from their work, but from the organization's ability to help them succeed. That disengagement rarely shows up in big moments. Instead, it emerges in the everyday: delays in approvals, mismatched expectations, silent frustrations. It creates a culture not of resistance, but of resignation.

Structural clarity doesn't remove complexity. But it gives complexity shape. It helps teams move with direction, confidence, and coherence. It turns improvisation into intentionality, and turns scattered effort into forward momentum.

Cross-Tier Impact

When the systems that are meant to support work are undefined, outdated, or inconsistently applied, the effects ripple far beyond **Tier 4**. Operational ambiguity isn't just a technical inconvenience. It becomes a barrier to trust, alignment, and organizational growth across all five tiers.

In **Tier 1**, the absence of operational clarity undermines even the strongest values. A commitment to "transparency" or "collaboration" becomes difficult to uphold when no one can explain how decisions are made or where responsibilities lie. Without defined processes, mission and values lose their grounding in daily behavior. They become aspirational rather than operational.

Tier 2 often bears the burden of these gaps. Leaders are forced to make decisions in a vacuum, each interpreting the "right way" through their own lens. Without shared systems, consistency across departments erodes. Strategic direction may remain intact at the highest levels, but its execution becomes uneven. The more leaders must improvise, the more strategy becomes personalized instead of organizational.

Tier 3, focused on people and culture, suffers quietly. Employees internalize structural ambiguity as a reflection of what the organization values. If processes are unclear or outdated, they don't just impact efficiency. They signal that clarity, support, and accountability may be negotiable. Onboarding becomes guesswork. Development stalls. Frustration grows not from uncertainty, not from workload.

In **Tier 5**, where feedback loops and continuous improvement are meant to thrive, invisible systems act like a fog. Even when employees provide valuable input, there's nowhere for it to land. Without a clear process for applying lessons learned, the organization struggles to retain insight. Momentum is lost not because people aren't learning, but because the structure doesn't know how to respond.

When **Tier 4** is neglected, the whole framework starts to strain. Operational clarity is not about micromanagement. It's about building a shared foundation, one that can hold purpose, support leadership, elevate people, and convert learning into movement.

Designing the Shift

Jordan understood that solving the problem wasn't about creating new rules. It was about uncovering the ones that already existed (spoken or not), and redesigning the ones that no longer served. The first step was visibility. Before an organization can fix its systems, it must first see them clearly.

He began by mapping workflows not from policy, but from behavior. He sat with teams and asked, "How do you actually get this done?" Not, "What's supposed to happen," but, "What do you do when it's 4:58 p.m. on a deadline and you need to move fast?"

What emerged was a revealing landscape of assumptions, improvisations, and informal fixes. The employee handbook, long outdated and misaligned, had become irrelevant. The real systems were silent and situational, shaped by workarounds rather than intention.

To shift this, Jordan introduced a Process Clarification Sprint. Over two weeks, small cross-functional teams traced one workflow each – onboarding, expense approval, scheduling time off – and answered five questions: Who owns this? Where does it begin? Where does it stall? What's missing? And who suffers when it breaks? These weren't audits. They were discovery missions.

Jordan didn't lead the sprints alone. He partnered with middle managers and front-line staff to co-create process maps that reflected the organization's true operating rhythm. Every ambiguity uncovered was treated as a design flaw to reimagine.

From these sessions, new systems began to emerge, not imposed, but built together. Clear documentation followed, written in plain language. Internal FAQs were created. Workflow diagrams were posted and updated. The handbook wasn't rewritten as a formality, it was redesigned as a living resource, tied to actual daily needs. And most importantly, every change was tested by the people who would use it.

This shift wasn't revolutionary in its scope, but it was transformational in its intention. Systems stopped being inherited and started being owned. Questions like "Who approves this?" and "Where do I find that?" no longer derailed momentum. Clarity became a cultural asset, not just an operational goal.

True systems change doesn't begin with software or policy. It begins with curiosity, collaboration, and the courage to admit when what's written doesn't match how work really gets done.

Operationalizing Change

Bringing visibility and consistency to an organization's workflows doesn't begin with massive overhauls. It begins with listening. Operational gaps are often embedded in day-to-day processes, quietly normalized over time.

The first step in reclaiming clarity is to create space for observation. Leaders should initiate a workflow discovery cycle, inviting cross-functional teams to map key operational processes from start to finish. This isn't about documenting what's supposed to happen, it's about understanding what actually happens, where confusion surfaces, and how workarounds have taken root.

From these conversations, ownership gaps typically emerge. When systems are invisible, it's often because no one is formally responsible for them. Each essential workflow should have a clear owner tasked with maintaining the process, updating documentation, and ensuring accessibility. Without defined accountability, even the best-designed systems lose relevance as the organization evolves.

Legacy tools such as outdated employee handbooks or procedural templates should be critically reviewed. These artifacts often remain untouched, their irrelevance only revealed when something breaks. Instead of clinging to policies for the sake of tradition, organizations must align operational guidance with present-day reality. Rewrite documents with simplicity, purpose, and usability in mind. Focus not just on the rules, but on the reasons behind them.

Documentation should also be treated as living guidance, not static files buried in shared drives. Visual aids, collaborative platforms, and clear language make processes easier to understand and adapt. Regular process health reviews can ensure that workflows remain efficient, aligned, and responsive to emerging needs. Just as performance evaluations should guide employee growth, workflow reviews can serve as a structured opportunity to reflect, recalibrate, and improve.

Operational clarity also requires cultural support. Employees need to be trained on how systems work and why they matter. By teaching staff to navigate systems with confidence and curiosity, organizations move from compliance to engagement. And when feedback surfaces, through pain points, questions, or ideas, it must be acknowledged and acted upon. Employees will stop offering insight if the system stops listening.

Most importantly, system redesign must be normalized. Changing how a process works should not feel like a failure, it should feel like maintenance. When organizations treat process improvement as an ongoing discipline rather than a reactive fix, they create space for agility. Momentum returns when employees no longer have to guess how to move forward, and instead are guided by systems that are built to serve, not slow, their work.

Executive Takeaways

Clarity is a leadership responsibility. When employees are forced to guess how systems work, when processes differ from one department to another, and when handbooks gather dust filled with outdated references, the result isn't just inefficiency. It's mistrust. Inconsistent systems send a quiet but powerful message: the organization isn't sure how it operates. And if the organization isn't sure, how can its people be?

The most effective leaders recognize that operational gaps are rarely the fault of individuals. They are the result of structure left unattended. When workarounds become the norm, when decision-making relies on hallway conversations or institutional memory, the system is no longer serving the mission. It's silently standing in the way of it.

This is not about implementing perfection. It's about creating systems that are navigable, transparent, and intentionally designed to evolve. Leaders should ask: Are our core workflows documented? Are they understood? Are they accessible and adaptable? And perhaps most importantly, who owns them?

To lead operational change is to accept that clarity is not a one-time deliverable. It is a habit. It is earned through regular conversation, thoughtful review, and the consistent invitation for feedback. By creating systems that are living, supported, and continuously improved, organizations not only reduce friction, they restore trust.

And trust is what allows people to stop working around the process and start moving with it.

Chapter 8: Leadership Checkpoints

- Where in your organization are workflows assumed but not clearly defined?
- Are employees frequently relying on memory, workaround habits, or informal knowledge to complete routine tasks?
- How often is your employee handbook reviewed, updated, and integrated into real-time practice?
- Do new hires receive consistent operational guidance, or does clarity depend on who trains them?
- Are there documented processes for cross-functional collaboration or do teams "figure it out" as they go?
- Who is responsible for maintaining process documentation, and is that role clearly defined and resourced?
- When systems break down or confusion arises, is the response reactive or are there mechanisms to surface and address systemic issues?
- What is one area of operational ambiguity you could clarify this quarter, and what ripple effects might that clarity create?

TIER 5:
IMPACT
& OUTCOMES

Driving Adaptation & Sustainable Growth

CHAPTER 9

THE STAGNANT GIANT

When Learning Stops

THE STORY OF TAMARA

Once, they had led the industry.

Atlas Technologies was a legacy name in logistics software, so embedded in the fabric of global distribution networks that it was often said clients didn't just use their tools, they built entire infrastructures around them. For over two decades, Atlas had been the standard. They expanded aggressively, acquired strategically, and refined their operations with the precision of a machine that seemed incapable of breaking down. When supply chains were a quiet whisper in business strategy, Atlas was already charting paths through them.

Their strength was in their predictability. Their edge, they believed, was institutional wisdom, an archive of success that gave them quiet confidence. Their executives wore that confidence like a crest. "We've seen it all," their CEO would say at town halls. "We know what works."

And then, almost imperceptibly at first, the ground began to shift.

Competitors, lean and curious, began to release platforms built for the cloud. They were intuitive, agile, even beautiful. These new players didn't just match Atlas's functionality; they reimagined it. They introduced predictive analytics, real-time dashboards, and AI-enhanced automation that eliminated entire categories of decision fatigue. Their interfaces made Atlas's clunky windows feel like museum artifacts.

But inside Atlas, change was not met with urgency. It was met with nostalgia. The top brass believed their edge was their depth, not their design. Middle managers learned to avoid the discomfort of challenging processes. Product teams stuck to incremental updates, careful not to disrupt "what had always worked." Training programs sat untouched on shared drives, older than the interns being hired. The last employee engagement survey had been conducted during a rebrand, then quietly buried.

Tamara, a rising engineer, once proposed a bold new integration that would bring Atlas's platform into real-time sync with several partner systems. It could reduce client workload by nearly 30%. She was thanked for her "passion" and told, gently, to stay focused on her core deliverables. She learned quickly: innovation without invitation was unwelcome.

The signs weren't cataclysmic. Clients didn't leave en masse, they just failed to renew. Talented employees didn't revolt, they quietly moved on. Performance didn't plummet, it plateaued. And in the boardroom, performance reviews still looked good. But outside, the world was changing.

Atlas wasn't failing. But it was stagnating. Still large. Still functional. But no longer curious. No longer learning. And inch by inch, the world was beginning to pass them by.

The Strategic Lens

The story of Atlas Technologies is not about failure. It's about forgetting. Forgetting how to learn. Forgetting that legacy alone cannot sustain relevance. But stagnation rarely announces itself. It settles in slowly, protected by the comfort of familiarity and disguised by the rhythm of routine.

To assess whether your organization is moving forward or quietly stalling, step outside the quarterly reports and surface metrics. Look instead at how the organization encounters and responds to disruption. Not just external disruption, but internal challenge. When a new idea is offered, is it explored or explained away? Are questions welcomed, or redirected? Does the structure make room for experimentation or punish it with indifference?

Begin by examining your organizational muscle for reflection. Do teams have the time and permission to pause and evaluate, beyond outcomes, to the path taken to get there? A performance culture that only measures delivery often misses its most valuable asset: insight.

Next, assess the visibility of learning. Are lessons learned publicly shared? Do other teams know what their peers are experimenting with? If improvement lives in isolated folders or stays locked in the minds of a few leaders, your organization is not yet learning systemically. It's learning accidentally.

Then consider the psychological safety embedded in your structure. Is failure framed as data, or danger? Do people whisper ideas in backchannels, or offer them confidently in front of peers? Curiosity cannot thrive in fear. And fear, when unspoken, often masquerades as professionalism.

Finally, evaluate your structures of accountability for learning. Does someone own continuous improvement, or is it assumed to just "happen"? Is reflection embedded into job roles, performance conversations, and strategic planning, or is it treated as a luxury for when there's time? Without infrastructure, even the best intentions will fade.

Stagnation isn't always visible on the surface. But when you zoom out, the signs are there: outdated metrics, unchallenged systems, long-tenured comfort zones, and a culture that rewards maintenance over movement.

The most important question is not, "Are we performing?"

The most important question is, "Are we still becoming?"

Structural Insights

Organizations don't collapse in a single, dramatic moment. They fade first through slow disengagement, subtle irrelevance, and the quiet erosion of learning. Stagnation is a dangerous organizational illness because it wears the costume of stability. When routines go unquestioned and innovation is treated as disruption rather than necessity, the organization may appear intact, but the engine has already begun to seize.

Continuous improvement is not an inspirational slogan. It's a structural discipline. It requires intentional systems that elevate reflection, reward adaptability, and ensure the organization learns not just in response to crisis, but as a matter of rhythm. Without those systems, insight remains siloed, feedback is dismissed or buried, and growth becomes incidental rather than designed.

The absence of learning is more than a cultural gap, it's a structural failure. When systems don't make space for experimentation or feedback, capable people either disengage or leave. What could have been transformative ideas are quietly deleted from drafts and never submitted. Projects are executed without retrospection. Metrics are reported without narrative. The message becomes clear: delivery matters more than discovery.

Stagnation doesn't always look like struggle. Sometimes it looks like a clean dashboard, a predictable calendar, a team that no longer asks why. And that is precisely what makes it so hard to catch, until it's too late.

Cross-Tier Impact

This chapter stands at the top of the *Five Tiers Framework* because it reflects whether all previous tiers are working together or have become misaligned. But **Tier 5** cannot function in isolation. Its success depends entirely on what has come before.

If **Tier 1** lacks clarity, if the organization does not know what its purpose is or what future it's trying to build, then improvement loses direction. Feedback gets collected, but no one knows what to do with it. Learning becomes sporadic, unmoored from mission.

In **Tier 2**, if leaders are not aligned around growth and adaptation, reflective practices remain isolated. One department might learn and iterate. Another might stick to old practices without challenge. This fragmented approach creates silos not just in work, but in wisdom.

Tier 3 brings in the people dimension. Culture plays a critical role in whether feedback is shared, whether learning is safe, and whether insight flows in all directions. If speaking up is risky or dismissed, then the organization will never know what it's capable of. Employees withhold ideas, feedback loops fail, and the learning ecosystem collapses.

In **Tier 4**, systems must be designed to support change, not resist it. When process redesign requires navigating a maze of approvals, improvement stalls. If tools are outdated or misaligned, innovation becomes exhausting rather than exciting. **Tier 4** gives learning a place to land. If that place is broken, insight has nowhere to go.

Tier 5 does not ask whether your organization is busy. It asks whether it is evolving. It is the test of integration, where voice, purpose, leadership, systems, and values converge. And if they don't, the organization begins to drift, slowly but surely, into irrelevance.

Designing the Shift

Bringing **Tier 5** to life begins with making learning not just acceptable, but expected. Organizations must treat improvement as a shared responsibility, not an occasional initiative. This means building time, structure, and visibility into how learning happens across every layer of the system.

Start by creating clear venues for reflection. This includes leadership retrospectives, project post-mortems, and team learning reviews, not just when things go wrong, but when things go well. Normalize asking: What worked? What didn't? What did we learn?

Feedback systems must be real, accessible, and multi-directional. Anonymous and open channels should coexist. Employees should have avenues to share upward, laterally, and across functions. And every feedback loop must include visible follow-up. "We heard you" is not enough. Showing action is where trust is built.

Learning should be embedded in routines, not tacked on. Strategic planning should include space for lessons learned. Performance reviews should include what someone has discovered, not just what they delivered. New employee onboarding should introduce not only systems, but how the organization adapts and grows.

Reward the behavior you want to see. Recognize the manager who adjusted course after feedback. Celebrate the team that shared a failed project publicly and made it a case study for improvement. Make it safe to say, "This didn't work." And make it valuable to say, "Here's what we're trying next."

Lastly, measure learning. Create dashboards or reports that track tasks completed and insights gained. Document what changed, why it changed, and what was learned. Over time, this creates an organizational memory that can be shared, built upon, and evolved.

Operationalizing Change

The first step is to embed a rhythm of reflection. Launch a quarterly cycle where every department answers the same set of simple questions: What did we try? What did we learn? What will we do differently? Publish these reflections internally, and build a culture of transparency around improvement.

Create a learning dashboard that includes metrics for experiments, changes implemented, and feedback loops closed. This shifts reporting from purely output-based to insight-based, signaling that learning is a key performance indicator (KPI).

Host regular "Failure Showcases," forums where teams can openly share what didn't work and what they learned from it. These moments dismantle the stigma around failure and reinforce the value of risk-taking in a supportive environment.

Appoint improvement stewards or continuous learning leads in each department. Their role is to ensure that feedback leads to learning, and that learning leads to action. They become the internal architects of reflection, helping to translate ideas into structures and habits.

And always return to the core question: Is your organization learning? And not just growing, or working, or producing, but actually learning. Because without learning, no organization can adapt. And without adaptation, no organization can survive the pivots of what may come next.

Executive Takeaways

Organizations do not stay strong by staying the same. They grow, they flex, they adapt. Or ... they fade. The tragedy of stagnation is not in collapse, but in the quiet erosion of potential. When learning stops, so does momentum. And eventually, so does the organization's relevance.

But learning can be reignited. With rhythm, systems, and a willingness to ask, "What's next," instead of "What's always worked," organizations can become engines of discovery. They can move not only with the market, but ahead of it.

Continuous improvement isn't just a tool for performance. Continuous improvement is a philosophy of aliveness. It is the belief that every challenge contains a lesson, every failure offers a pivot, and every voice has something worth hearing.

Chapter 9: Leadership Checkpoints

- What formal structures currently support learning in your organization, and where are the gaps?
- How is feedback tracked, shared, and followed through from insight to action?
- Are people in your organization recognized for what they learn, or only for what they accomplish?
- When was the last time your team paused to reflect on a process, a result, or a mistake?
- What is one structural change you could make this quarter to turn reflection into routine?

CHAPTER 10

BUILDING WHAT'S NEXT

Leading With Curiosity & Intention

THE STORY OF NICOLETTE

No one expected her to succeed.

Nicolette Harper was young, perhaps too young, some whispered, for the CEO seat of a long-established construction firm whose name once carried weight in city contracts, public infrastructure, and regional planning boards. For decades, the company had been the go-to for solid, dependable work. But over the years, as newer competitors emerged with more nimble pricing, smarter tech integrations, and sleeker operations, the edge dulled. Clients hadn't vanished, but the contracts had shrunk. Projects once celebrated now just met minimums. Internally, employee energy had settled into a kind of quiet resignation. People did their jobs, but without the spark that once made them proud to wear the company's gear. Profits were stable, but purpose had flatlined.

When Nicolette stepped into the role, she didn't arrive with bold slogans or sweeping declarations. She didn't promise transformation or talk about "disruption." Instead, she brought a notebook and an honest curiosity. On her very first day, she visited three job sites. Not for a photo op or to check compliance, but to listen. She crouched beside a backhoe operator and asked, "What's the biggest thing that slows you down?" She asked a site manager what decisions he couldn't make on his own and why. In the office, she asked HR how long it really took to onboard a new hire, and what fell through the cracks. She visited finance and sat quietly as they walked her through outdated approval systems. She asked procurement why it took three weeks to order a $12 wrench.

At first, the questions raised eyebrows. CEOs didn't usually ask these things. Some assumed she was hunting for inefficiencies to cut. Others suspected it was a show for the board. But then something happened that hadn't happened in years: she started responding. And not with memos, but with action. She didn't go after the biggest reforms first. Instead, she focused on smaller things, easily fixable frustrations that had piled up into cultural weight. Procurement systems were cleaned up. Onboarding was streamlined. Communication channels were clarified. And each time something shifted, she connected the change to the question that had uncovered it.

Within months, employees began volunteering their ideas. Nicolette launched a cross-functional initiative called "Build Forward," where anyone, from site techs to legal assistants, could submit process improvements, backed by the assurance that the best would be implemented. She introduced monthly learning circles, not led by consultants, but by employees from different departments, with different realities, who began sharing how their work intersected and where misalignments lived. She didn't chase a rebrand or hire an innovation team. She simply made learning the default mode. She rebuilt the company, not by rewriting its identity, but by reigniting its sense of purpose and responsiveness.

In doing so, Nicolette didn't just lead a comeback. She initiated a quiet renaissance. The company didn't transform through a strategic pivot. It evolved through presence. Curiosity. Intention. It wasn't about rebuilding what had once worked. It was about building what would work next.

The Strategic Lens

The transformation led by Nicolette wasn't born from disruption, it was born from design. Not grand redesigns, but intentional calibration. The lesson for any organization isn't in her title, it's in her posture. Curiosity became a leadership tool. Active listening became a strategic function. And responsiveness became the pulse of the firm's culture.

To step back and assess whether your organization is building what's next, or merely maintaining what's now, start by observing how questions move within your system. Are they welcomed, elevated, and answered, or do they disappear into the ether of hierarchy and habit? The health of your strategy is not just measured by its clarity, but by its capacity to evolve through honest dialogue.

Examine where decisions live. Are they centralized, distant from the work, or do they reflect a structure where those closest to the challenge have a say in shaping the solution? An organization that fears frontline insight is one that slowly starves itself of relevance.

Reflect on how your systems interpret time. Is urgency always tied to crisis? Or have you created intentional space for preemptive adaptation, spaces where teams can pause, reflect, and recalibrate before problems scale? Responsive systems are proactive, not performative.

Next, evaluate whether experimentation is visible and valued. When a new idea is tested, is it shared? When something doesn't work, is it studied or buried? Learning organizations normalize trial and error, not to celebrate failure, but to cultivate fluency in forward motion.

Finally, ask whether your strategy lives in motion. Does it invite participation? Is it revisited as conditions change, or does it rest untouched, guarded by tradition and formality? A living strategy isn't unstable, it's alive. And aliveness, in today's climate, is its own form of strength.

The organizations that endure are not the ones that resist change longest. They're the ones that learn how to shape it with humility, clarity, and intention. They're the ones that stay close to their people and close to the ground because that's where the next direction often rises first.

Structural Insights

Resilient organizations don't survive by locking in a perfect plan. They survive by designing for movement. They survive with strategic responsiveness rooted in clarity, grounded in values, and animated by curiosity. The most successful organizations don't bet on certainty; they bet on their ability to sense, interpret, and adapt. They don't react only when change becomes urgent. They make reflection and responsiveness part of their structure.

Strategic alignment, in this context, is not rigidity. It is the spine through which movement becomes purposeful. Without anchoring to **Tier 1**, any attempt at innovation becomes untethered. But alignment alone is not enough. Long-term success also requires adaptive systems, flexible leadership, and cultures that welcome experimentation as a learning process rather than a risk to be avoided.

Nicolette's approach worked because it respected the foundational tiers while activating the top. In **Tier 2**, leadership was empowered not just to maintain status, but to lead through change. In **Tier 3**, culture was shifted from one of quiet compliance to one of shared ownership. Employees no longer waited for directives, they contributed to direction. In **Tier 4**, outdated systems were not tolerated as historical artifacts; they were evaluated and redesigned with the people who used them most. And in **Tier 5**, feedback wasn't a quarterly survey, it was a living system that informed decisions in real time.

Resilience, then, is not a result. It is a capability. And that capability can be cultivated by asking better questions, designing smarter systems, and building organizations that stay curious about themselves and the world they serve.

Cross-Tier Impact

Tier 5: Impact & Outcomes can only function if the other four tiers are alive and integrated. Strategic responsiveness begins in **Tier 1**, where clarity of purpose creates a filter for all action. If an organization doesn't know why it exists or who it serves, it cannot respond meaningfully to change. Nicolette didn't start with vision statements; she uncovered the values that had been buried beneath bureaucracy, and used them to reawaken a sense of shared direction.

In **Tier 2**, leadership alignment ensures that improvement is allowed and, more importantly, expected. Leaders who model inquiry and respond visibly set the tone for the rest of the system. Under Nicolette's guidance, department heads began modeling her behavior and that mirrored curiosity rippled outward.

Tier 3 is the cultural engine. A culture that reinforces reflection, ownership, and shared contribution allows responsiveness to scale. When employees see their ideas being taken seriously, acted upon, and publicly recognized, they internalize a belief that their voice matters. The shift from passive to participatory culture is subtle, but powerful.

Tier 4 ensures that operational systems don't sabotage progress. Change dies when it hits processes that can't bend. Nicolette didn't demand agility, she built for it. She invested in systems and policies that could support adaptation, not obstruct it.

And **Tier 5**, at its best, becomes the dashboard of organizational health, not just reporting performance, but revealing capacity for movement, learning, and growth.

Designing the Shift
To lead with curiosity and intention is to lead in motion. This begins with reframing strategy as something living, not a 5-year plan laminated and locked away, but a tool that evolves in response to insight. Strategic plans must contain room for adjustment, room for learning, and room for co-creation.

Nicolette demonstrated this by involving employees in the strategic rewrite. This was done as a belief: those closest to the work often hold the clearest view of what needs to shift.

Organizations should institutionalize review rhythms, quarterly cycles where insights are gathered, discussed, and implemented. These reviews should involve leaders and representatives from every tier of the organization, building a practice of listening across distance.

Decision-making frameworks must also be clarified. Empowerment is meaningless without guardrails. Employees should know what they can change, what they can influence, and what needs escalation. This reduces friction, builds confidence, and accelerates action.

Leaders must be trained in sense-making – how to interpret weak signals, recognize trends, and act before crisis. This requires both individual skill and system support: data dashboards, pulse checks, and employee insights that are reviewed weekly, monthly, continuously.

Lastly, resiliency indicators must be integrated into performance tracking. These indicators should measure more than efficiency. They should evaluate adaptability, cross-functional collaboration, time to decision, team health, and engagement in improvement efforts. In doing so, the organization begins to treat flexibility as a core competency.

Operationalizing Change
Begin by creating a shared rhythm for inquiry. Launch structured reflection sessions at every level, asking teams to regularly consider: What's working? What's unclear? What should we change next? These questions build a culture of reflection into the operational cadence.

Establish learning circles or cross-functional "strategy sprints" where teams explore opportunities, run small experiments, and share results. These efforts don't require formal innovation labs, just space, permission, and support.

Track leadership responsiveness. Develop an internal curiosity index, a measure of how often employee input is gathered and acted on. Track decisions made and feedback addressed. This builds accountability for responsiveness, not just output.

Create a living "What's Next" playbook. This is an evolving document that captures improvement cycles, feedback themes, and emerging goals. Make it accessible, participatory, and iterative. Let it be a mirror and a compass.

And above all, teach leaders to ask better questions.

Curiosity is not weakness. It is strategic strength.

Executive Takeaways

The organizations that thrive in the years ahead won't be those with the most data, or even the most resources. They'll be the ones that can move. Those who learn, reflect, respond, and reimagine. The ones that treat feedback as direction, not distraction. The ones that ask, listen, and adapt with integrity.

To build what's next, we must first stop trying to recreate what was. Progress lives in presence. Strategy lives in conversation. And leadership, at its best, is less about having all the answers and more about creating the conditions where better answers emerge.

In a world of uncertainty, responsiveness becomes the new resilience. And the future doesn't arrive with clarity – it arrives with questions.

Chapter 10: Leadership Checkpoints

- Does your organization's current strategy make space for learning and iteration, or is it overly fixed?
- How do leaders in your company demonstrate curiosity, and how is it rewarded?
- Are decisions made too far from where the work happens? What would happen if they weren't?
- How does your organization track or respond to environmental shifts, market feedback, or internal suggestions?
- What's one practice, policy, or mindset you could let go of today in order to make room for growth tomorrow?

CONCLUSION

THE FLOW FORWARD

CONCLUSION: THE FLOW FORWARD

This is not easy work. Nor will it ever be. Let's start there. This is not to discourage you, but to honor the truth of what lies ahead. This is about creating expectation. This may also seem somewhat idealistic. And perhaps it is. Perhaps this is too much of an undertaking, especially with already having to balance an overwhelmed calendar.

But building an organization that is not only functional, but foundationally sound and future-ready, is a long and demanding process. It requires more than leadership charisma or a well-articulated plan. It asks for structural courage. For honest reflection. For a willingness to face the ways in which even well-intentioned systems can drift into dysfunction, and for the discipline to keep going anyway.

But difficulty is not the enemy. Drift is. Drifting into default. Into tradition for tradition's sake. Into outdated systems, misaligned leadership, and hollow culture. The organizations that will survive are the ones that resist drift. They don't wait for crisis to change. They choose movement. They choose alignment. And most importantly, they choose to build forward.

The *Five Tiers Framework* offers that choice. It offers it not as a shortcut, but a structured path. It begins with **Tier 1: Foundational Core**, the living heart of any organization. This is not about a catchy mission statement or a slide buried in onboarding decks. It's about anchoring the entire system to purpose, vision, values, and governance. When **Tier 1** is strong, it's felt. Decisions make sense. Policies reinforce culture. Employees know what they're part of, and *why* it matters. When it's weak, the symptoms are subtle but unmistakable: conflict without resolution, passion without direction, effort without cohesion. A scattered mission leads to a scattered organization. So, we start here, not because it's glamorous, but because it's essential.

And once the foundation is set, we move to **Tier 2: Leadership & Strategy**, where the abstract becomes operational. Leadership alignment is often romanticized as visionary retreats or consensus-driven dialogue. But in practice, it's much harder, and much more structural. It requires defining how leaders function as a system, not as isolated experts. Do they understand their shared priorities? Do they model the organization's values when the pressure is on? Do their strategies complement each other, or compete silently beneath the surface? When leaders pull in the same direction, strategy becomes more than a document. It becomes muscle memory. Without it, even the clearest vision crumbles under the weight of misalignment.

That alignment cascades directly into **Tier 3: Culture & People**, the living pulse of the organization. Culture is not created by perks or policies. Culture is shaped by patterns. By who gets rewarded. By how mistakes are handled. By whether employees feel safe enough to speak truth, and valued enough to stay. Organizations often say they value integrity, collaboration, or inclusion, but those values only matter if they're reflected in behavior, especially in moments of tension. A strong culture is not one that avoids conflict, but one that can hold it with care. When people know where they stand, what they're a part of, and how they can grow, culture becomes a force of forward motion. But when culture is left to chance, it calcifies. And once calcified, it begins to break.

Which brings us to **Tier 4: Processes & Systems**, where good intentions rise or fall. The best leaders and most passionate teams cannot succeed within broken systems. When workflows are needlessly complex, when approval chains stretch into weeks, when technology frustrates rather than supports, the organization becomes exhausting. Not because the mission isn't worthy, but because the infrastructure cannot carry the weight of it. In **Tier 4**, the question is not "Are we productive," but, "Is the system designed for clarity, efficiency, and flow?" This is where the friction lives, and where it must be released. Streamlined processes are not just operational wins. They are cultural affirmations that people's time, energy, and insight matter.

Finally, we arrive at **Tier 5: Impact & Outcomes**, the culmination and test of every tier before it. Here, we examine whether the organization is not just functioning, but learning. Whether it is evolving, reflecting, and responding in real time. This is where improvement becomes structural rather than performative. Feedback loops must close visibly. Reflection must be normalized in failure and in success. Continuous improvement cannot be a seasonal initiative. It must be the rhythm of the organization. Because in the end, it's not what you do once that defines you. It's what you make a habit of. **Tier 5** turns those habits into capability, so that every insight becomes action, every mistake becomes data, and every challenge becomes an opportunity for growth.

Taken together, the five tiers are not a checklist. They are an ecosystem. Each tier feeds the next. A weak foundation undermines leadership. Poor leadership fractures culture. Disconnected culture erodes systems. Broken systems block feedback. And feedback without integration is just noise. But when aligned, when each tier reinforces and reflects the others, you don't just build a better organization. You build an organization capable of becoming better, continuously.

And that's the promise.

No, it won't be easy. But that doesn't mean it's not possible. In fact, it's more possible now than ever, because you are here, reading this, asking the questions most leaders avoid. That alone puts you ahead. You don't need to be perfect. You don't need to change everything at once. But you do need to begin. Choose one policy to revisit. One leadership conversation to have. One cultural behavior to start modeling. One system to clean up. One loop to close. The flow forward isn't built in leaps. It's built in layers.

So take a breath. Then take the next step.

Because the future of your organization isn't waiting on better timing. It's waiting on better structure. Better questions. Better flow.

You're not just managing what is. You're shaping what could be.

This is your invitation to build what's next with purpose, with courage, and with the conviction that the hard path is often the right one.

Let it begin. Let it be hard. And let it be worth it.

Let it flow forward.

ABOUT THE AUTHOR

Kenneth Pearson has always believed that knowledge isn't meant to be hoarded, it's meant to be shared. Across every role he's held, every organization he's supported, and every quiet moment of reflection, his passion has remained the same: to take what he's learned and offer it in ways that help others grow, lead, and live with more intention.

As Co-Founder and Organizational Development Consultant at *Pearson & Pearson LLC*, Kenneth works alongside startups, nonprofits, tribal government agencies, and mission-driven teams to design systems that work and make sense. His focus is never just the fix. It's the transfer of wisdom, the shaping of mindset, the building of trust and internal capacity, so that when he steps away, what remains is strong, clear, and wholly the organization's own.

He is also the Creator and Program Designer of *Live a Haiku Life*, a philosophy and practice grounded in simplicity, presence, and the power of noticing. It's a way of living and leading that informs much of Kenneth's work, including his writing and facilitation.

Through *Unboxing OD*, his podcast on organizational development, and *Quiet Currents*, his exploration of haiku and mindful leadership, Kenneth opens doors for others to think more deeply, act more gently, and lead more authentically.

Additionally, Kenneth holds a Master of Science in Industrial Organizational Psychology and an MFA in Creative Writing. His work moves at the intersection of structure and soul, strategy and story. For him, the real measure of impact isn't in the noise made, but in the clarity left behind.

He lives in Southern Arizona with his wife, Cory Lynn. On the weekends, you might find him reading before sunrise, spending time with his wife and pets, or walking desert trails where the silence speaks just loud enough.

The Flow of Five Tiers is more than a framework. It's intended to be an offering, a reflection, and a call to build something lasting by beginning where all transformation does ...

... with good intentions!

As always, thank you for reading!

If you would like to learn more about Kenneth

& *The Flow of Five Tiers*,

you can do so by visiting the following websites:

LinkedIn

www.linkedin.com/in/kenneth-pearson

Pearson & Pearson LLC

www.pearsonpearson.llc

Live a Haiku Life

www.liveahaikulife.com